LEADERSHIP: THE JOURNEY INWARD

Second Edition

Delorese Ambrose, Ed.D.

KENDALL/HUNT PUBLISHING COMPANY
4050 Westmark Drive   Dubuque, Iowa 52002

Dedication

For my family, circle of friends, and clients who encourage me to model the way.

C O N T E N T S

P R E F A C E

I wrote *Leadership: The Journey Inward* in 1991 as an outgrowth of my personal fascination with the art and science of leadership, and in an attempt to document my growing understanding of the subject. The response from readers has been most encouraging. The book has reached a broad audience: from corporate leadership seminars in Fortune 500 companies to volunteers in the Association of Junior Leagues International; from Langley High School in Pittsburgh to the University of Cairo in Egypt.

The positive reactions to *The Journey Inward* far exceeded my expectations. In addition, I received helpful feedback and ideas from many readers. These have shaped this second edition.

I have reworked and renamed Chapter 1 to focus on "A New Context for Leadership." The former Chapter 8, "Creating A Motivating Environment," has been incorporated into the discussion of leadership and followership in Chapter 4 of the new edition. I have expanded the "Life Lessons" exercise and renamed it "Life Mapping" to reflect the new focus on critical **life events** and associated feelings, **key persons** and their impact, and critical **personal choices** and the results. This, more in-depth experience now appears earlier in the book under the revised Chapter 3: Self Knowledge: Prerequisite for Leadership. Finally, I have added new examples of leadership, and **a summary of steps for "Moving Inward" and "Moving Outward"** at the end of the book.

I hope you find this edition even more useful than the first.

Delorese Ambrose, Ed. D.
Pittsburgh, Pennsylvania, February, 1995

PART

UNDERSTANDING LEADERSHIP

A New Context for Leadership

As global values clash, families "re-define," governments "re-invent," and businesses "re-engineer," our attention rivets on a major concern: *Do we have the vision and the skills to secure our future?* From kindergarten to graduate school, in corporate seminar rooms and labor force training programs, in social service agencies and religious conferences, my clients seek new leadership skills. They now view leadership development as central to a well-rounded individual and key to our survival. They recognize that the best laid managerial plans will fail if they are not guided by leaders who have the character and skills to *re-establish trust and enable people* to execute the plans. Managerial and technical training are still important to ensure well-run organizations, but my clients in business, government, and the not-for-profit sector have become more concerned with how to educate and develop *a new breed of leaders* at all organizational levels.

This is not surprising. For decades, caught up in the daily tactical concerns of competitive growth, we have erred on the side of being short-sighted. Our environment, our economy, and our children now pay the price of our "quick fix" choices of the past. Blinded by a quest for world dominance and power, leaders in every sector have sacrificed long-term effectiveness for short-term "wins," preoccupied, in Warren Bennis' words, with "doing things right," rather than "doing the right things." The costs have been high. Current organizational efforts aimed at quality, process re-engineering, downsizing, school reform, reinventing government, multi-national partnerships, multi-cultural sensitivity, work/family balance, and environmental protection acknowledge our errors of the past and our concern for the future. As we move into an age of endless personal and global dilemmas, we must become creative architects of an uncertain future. Clearly we seek a new breed of leaders.

In this book I use the term "leader" to describe **anyone who inspires and promotes positive change, by engaging followers or enabling them to exercise leadership in their own right**. Effective leaders are motivated not just by their own purpose, but take into account the needs of others as well. By this definition, leadership and followership are inextricably linked. The two are connected not only because leaders must be guided by followers' concerns, but because it is the followers' perception of the leader's character and skills that determines the level of trust, and therefore the willingness to engage. Followers, in a sense, empower leaders to lead simply by deciding to follow! Where there is no followership—no demonstrated change— there is no leadership. Where there is no leadership—no demonstrated trustworthiness and competence—there is no followership.

My work with leadership over the past 17 years has shown me that leaders can emerge at any level in an organization, or in any walk of life. Holding a position of high status does not necessarily make someone a leader. Being an operative at the lowest rung of the organizational ladder does not necessarily prevent one from leading. While there is still an important role for formal leaders who create and manage organizations, smart executives include all members in a shared leadership process, where everyone's talents and perspectives are deployed to deliver quality goods and services.

This understanding of the leader/follower connection is critical today. We now live in a climate where the meaning of family, education, workplace, marketplace and community is challenged and changing rapidly. As these shifts have occurred, followers and leaders have experienced broken promises and a loss of trust. To regain our footing and secure the future we want, we must forge new leader/follower relationships. Let's take a more detailed look at the sweeping changes in values, educational needs, government, politics, world economics, family and community concerns that are shaping this new context for leadership.

◆ Worker values are changing from dependence and company loyalty to independence and personal choice. The concepts of "employee leadership," "ownership," and shared decision-making at all levels are taking hold as employees are encouraged to have input into shaping the organization's future. This is related to competitive trends that call for a focus on service excellence and quality, as well as lifestyle integration and job satisfaction for the employee.

◆ Education reform and school-to-work transition are becoming top priorities for both schools and big business. About one million young people drop out of U.S. high schools each year. Of the roughly 2.4 million who graduate, 25 percent are functionally illiterate; that is, they are unable to read and write at the eighth-grade level. At the same time, the growing "information economy" requires more educated and more highly-skilled workers. We see a growing trend towards community grassroots leadership in this arena as educators, unions, businesses, and employees themselves begin to create local, national, and international partnerships for change.

◆ Repressive forms of government are rapidly giving way to direct or semi-direct democracy in country after country. In an unimaginable turn of events, Nelson Mandela emerged as president of a country whose racist government imprisoned him for years. In the United States, people who formerly relegated their care to government are beginning to question the efficacy of doing so. We have shifted our stance vis-a-vis government as we focus increasingly on self-help and autonomy.

◆ The base of our economy has shifted from land development and manufacturing to information technology and services. We have moved from a narrow, national focus to a wide, global focus, both economically and socially. The basic premises of our culture's industrial paradigm are challenged as new technology reels forth faster than we can process it.

◆ Family issues redefine our political, social, and economic agenda, as we are forced to address new crises connected with health care, adult daycare, teen pregnancies, youth crime, and early childhood education.

◆ Diversity has emerged as one of the most critical issues in the '90s workplace. We have come to realize that our lack of sensitivity and skill in dealing with differences will have serious organizational consequences unless we learn to value and manage diversity. We now understand that the most competitive corporate leaders will be those who create a work environment where people can bring the very best they have to offer—

regardless of their family status, job classification, gender, race, age, creed, sexual orientation, physical attributes or abilities, socioeconomic status, or country of birth.

As "followers" we are more vocal about our need for quality leadership as we seek leaders who are trustworthy, flexible, and creative, and who value diversity and can build coalitions. In fact, many social scientists now claim that our planet's very survival may depend on our ability to produce a new breed of highly ethical, participative leaders at all levels: from the loftiest reaches of business and government, to grassroots community organizations and families. This awareness may well account for our present preoccupation with public scrutiny of those who choose to lead, be they CEO or politician, evangelist or parent.

Clearly, we must shift our position from our present focus on short-term goals to long-term thinking; from maintaining today's status quo to creating the future we desire; from depending on institutions to self-reliance; from competition to partnerships. This book was written to help you prepare for these new leadership challenges. It is designed as a self-study course that will allow you to draw on your own life experiences to develop your capacity to exercise leadership in different areas of your life, in different situations. The concepts and exercises presented apply equally to public sector, private sector, or personal leadership efforts. They should be useful to both the emerging and the seasoned leader. They apply to the act of "managing" and to the act of "leading."

Managing versus Leading

It is important at this point to understand this distinction between managing and leading, for there is a place for both, and the effective manager or leader must recognize when to use each.

Management aims at **maintenance**. The effective manager ensures that organizational goals are met efficiently and profitably, with a minimal amount of disruption. The same applies in personal or family life. When we manage our lives effectively, we keep things in balance; we are on top of the day-to-day demands.

Leadership aims at **change**. The effective leader inspires and empowers others to respond to challenges by using their creativity to secure the best possible future for all concerned. Similarly, when we exercise leadership in our personal lives, we work through crises creatively and push ourselves and perhaps others to new levels of effectiveness.

This is a book about leadership development. We will focus first on your **journey inward** to explore how your life experiences and the resulting personal choices may be linked to leadership. We will examine the capacity of ordinary people to exercise leadership in everyday situations, at work or at home, in the community or in personal endeavors. Through self-reflective exercises, you will examine the critical life events that have brought you to wherever you are right now, and the patterns of thought that govern your feelings and actions. This will allow you to discover potential barriers and gateways to your personal development, and identify ways to "let go" and be more open to the risks and choices necessary to unblock your path to more effective leadership.

Our focus will then shift to **the journey outward**. You will explore ways to direct the insights gained through self-reflection to your work with others, in whatever situation you choose. We will explore how you can develop your leadership potential by clarifying your own life purpose, how that purpose fits into your chosen work, your lifestyle and the groups you belong to.

My hope is that through this book you will create and claim your own leadership path. While I will offer you many examples of how world-renowned leaders emerge and perform, I provide these only because they are people whose leadership stories we may have all heard. These are simply recognizable examples, not recipes for you to follow mechanically. Everyday acts of leadership and followership are based on the same principles as monumental recorded acts of leadership. The goal is for you to find and celebrate your own unique way of leading, while you apply an awareness of the conditions and attributes that others like you have tapped when they chose or were chosen to lead. Keep in mind that whether you are a parent or businessperson, short-order cook or senator, you make leadership choices, or are chosen, based on your life struggles and experiences. By examining those experiences—and the strengths and perspectives each has taught you—you create your own blueprint for continued leadership development with more clarity and confidence.

How Leaders Emerge

M̲ost books about leadership focus on the journey outward. They examine the activities and style of established leaders in order to understand how leadership works. They then offer useful guidelines on the practices and skills of leadership. There still remains the largely unanswered question of how leadership develops in the first place, and what "ordinary" people can do to hone their leadership skills.

Why, for example, do some people choose to lead while others follow —or still others do neither? Does one have to be a great person to be considered a leader? If so, what is the source of this "greatness"? Is it innate or inborn? Is it inspired by parents or mentors? Is it a function of intelligence, or is it mere grit?

Early in my career, in an attempt to learn as much about leadership as I could, I read about those whose leadership successes were well documented. My students and I studied the lives of exemplary leaders like Gandhi, Mother Teresa, John F. Kennedy, Marcus Garvey, Winston Churchill, Golda Meir, Florence Nightingale, Martin Luther King, Jr.,

Moses, and Einstein. We were surely looking in the right places to find the great lessons of leadership. But we often used limited lenses, focusing on notables from the distant past, and too narrowly on questions about their leadership approaches. We explored the shared characteristics of great leaders, the reasons for their successes, what attracted followers to them, and most important, how to emulate them or learn from them, as we studied how to become effective leaders. These questions were, and still are, important to ask. They gave us many valuable insights into leadership. However, the most critical insight was not what I expected.

It is quite simply this: there are few, if any, universal paths to leadership. Sometimes leadership emerges from the ranks of nobility; at other times, it emerges from the squalor of poverty. Some leaders were reared by parents who inspired and supported them to do and be their best; others had their resolve to lead shaped by abusive parents.

When an ordinary person exercises extraordinary leadership—inspiring others to do or be more, changing the course of events in small communities, or in history, it is usually because of one or both of the following reasons:

1. The individual has made a fundamentally personal choice to influence his or her situation. For some this is a decision to act with integrity: to do the right thing in order to make a difficult situation better. For others the motive may be much more self-serving; they may want to be seen as powerful or effective in the world. In either case, if followers are attracted to the leader's vision, the person who chooses to lead has an impact.

2. Followers choose the leader. They notice something he or she is doing, or they perceive attributes of the would-be leader that they find attractive. They then decide to either follow the individual's lead, or press that person into leadership. As one

writer on leadership put it, if you look over your shoulder and people are following, you are a leader.

Rosa Parks exercised leadership when she decided, weary and worn out, to do the right thing on a bus in Montgomery, Alabama on her way home from work one evening. The management team of Johnson & Johnson exercised leadership when, in the aftermath of the Tylenol scare, they chose to do the right thing: be honest with the media and public, and directly confront the problem of their tainted, over-the-counter medication. (And, in the end, they gained customers due to their integrity.)

And there are countless other examples every day: Jennifer Daniels, a teenage mother of two, exercised leadership when, after putting herself through college at night, she decided to spend her time counseling and encouraging other teen parents to pursue their dreams; Mahatma Gandhi decided to stand up against the social injustices that blocked his path to career success; Samuel Gordon, an eighth-grade dropout, took on two jobs to move his family to a safer neighborhood and put each of his six children through college; Benazir Bhutto, in her moment of personal crisis, decided to continue her father's work and adopt his political responsibilities in a culture where few, if any, women possess such power; Dr. Sandra Murray, a young black scientist, nurtured an interest in anatomy and cell biology that took her from the South Side of Chicago to international prominence in her field; and Mikhail Gorbachev and Ronald Reagan decided to take a different approach, ending the Cold War. Some of these people's leadership actions have been duly noted in the pages of history. Others will never be written about, except in this brief paragraph. All have one thing in common:

These ordinary human beings chose to have an extraordinary impact on the situations in which they found themselves. In the words of Eleanor Roosevelt, they decided it was "better to light a candle than to curse the darkness."

As I discuss in Chapter 5, there are also vast differences in the styles of leaders. Some are shy and retiring, not given to oratorical brilliance or political maneuvering, while others thrive on these qualities. Some attract followers by listening and responding, others by vehement, forceful persuasion. In fact, I have come to believe that there are as many leadership paths as there are leaders!

In the end, the common thread that binds all leaders is that their emergence into leadership came about as they tried to resolve personal life crises, or dilemmas of choice in their organizations or communities. Each of the leaders cited thus far was trying to make sense of his or her world, and in the process engaged others in trying to change the world. Each could just as easily have chosen to succumb to the challenges life presented them, but chose instead to exercise personal and/or organizational power.

Leadership begins and ends with the internal development struggles of the individual leader. It is by integrating and learning from these crises that we gain the stamina and tools of effective leadership. In short, our blueprint for leadership is imbedded in our own life story. Winston Churchill understood this well when, upon being called into leadership of the British war effort, he commented that "All of my life experiences have prepared me for this hour."

We all embody leadership potential. That is, each of us is capable of influencing people and situations. Choosing to exercise this potential or demonstrating effective leadership behaviors varies by the individual and the circumstances he or she faces. Often, our decision to lead arises out of a personal crisis. In the process of figuring out how to cope with crises, we may strengthen our leadership qualities, and use these merits to creatively solve these situations and move forward. In the process of this resolution, we sometimes engage others, thereby exercising "leadership."

At times we are pressed into leadership by others—our children, our employers, our communities. These "followers" may call forth our talents because they admire the stand we have taken, or qualities we exhibit. Or they may simply decide to emulate the actions we take as we successfully wrestle with challenges. The would-be leader ultimately makes the personal choice to rise to the occasion. Folklore has it that Martin Luther King, Jr. did not explicitly set out to lead the Civil Rights Movement. Circumstances called forth his leadership when he was selected by followers who decided that his gifts of eloquence, his philosophy, and his impact on others were needed to address the racial crises of the moment.

The following are examples of the evolution of leadership out of personal struggles. I have selected people who became famous, and therefore known to most readers. However, this does not negate the capacity of each of us to lead in our own right. Like each of us, these leaders were faced with resolving personal needs—of avenging self-respect. As you read these accounts, I invite you to reflect on times when you experienced injustice or felt strongly about changing a situation.

Rosa Parks, who is regarded by many as an important civil rights leader, epitomizes the meaning of this book. What Mrs. Parks did, quite simply, was to decide—in a moment of personal crisis—that she had reached the end of her rope! Her decision to **empower herself, to finally do the right thing,** in a situation she had endured for countless years, underscores **the nature of leadership as an act of courage**.

Tired from a long day's work, and from years of racial discrimination that forced her to live with the daily humiliation of having to give up her seat to whites, she finally confronted her moment of crisis, leaned in, and emerged a leader. Hers is a dramatic example of how a seemingly insignificant woman ignited an entire movement by a single act of personal power. She describes her actions and feelings in a recent interview compiled by Brian Lanker:

> When he saw that I was still remaining in the seat, the driver said "If you don't stand up, I'm going to call the police and have you arrested." I said, "You may do that."

> Two policemen came and wanted to know what was the trouble. One said, "Why don't you stand up?" I said, "I don't think I should have to." At that point I asked the policeman, "Why do you push us around?" He said, "I don't know, but the law is the law and you're under arrest."

Mrs. Parks then goes on to offer an interesting account of leadership by example, and the relationship of followership, leadership, and personal power:

> People just stayed off the buses because I was arrested, not because I asked them [to]. If everybody else had been happy and doing well, my arrest wouldn't have made any difference at all . . . there was a kind of lifting of a burden from me individually. I could feel that whatever my individual desires were to be free, I was not alone . . . Many whites, even white Southerners, told me that even though it may have seemed like the blacks were being freed (by my actions), they felt more free and at ease themselves. They thought that my action didn't just free blacks, but them too.

This account, and the ones that follow, highlight three important observations about the emergence of leadership:

1. **You do not have to willfully set out to "be a leader" in order to exercise leadership**. If you demonstrate courage, honesty, integrity, and conviction in the way you go about resolving personal and interpersonal crises, you will sometimes emerge as a leader if people find your actions engaging.

2. **Followers empower leaders to lead**. It is the followers' perception that ultimately determines the scope of the leader's influence.

3. **When confronted with choice points in our lives, the direction we choose will determine whether we exercise leadership—creating the future we desire—or succumb to the pressure**. Also, whether we choose to lead or succumb depends on a variety of factors such as the circumstance, the people involved, our state of mind, our prior experiences and level of expertise, and our needs and motivations at the moment of choice.

Lech Walesa **outwardly demonstrated his personal resolve** when he scaled a 12-foot high wall into the Lenin shipyard to start the first of his now famous sit-ins on behalf of the Solidarity Labor Union members. Again, his struggle was, at its core, a **personal one**. While Lech Walesa is the first to admit that he was chosen by his followers, **his personal indignation fueled his need** to create a completely free Poland.

Corazon Aquino, a well-educated woman, was reportedly very content with her role of mother and statesman's devoted wife. She had no personal aspirations for the presidency of the Philippines. However, in wrestling with her personal life crisis—how to resolve the assassination of her husband—she reached inward, tapping her **courage** and the lessons her life experiences had taught her over the years. In a critical moment, she decided that the path she must take; the right thing to do under the circumstances was to carry forward her husband's work by becoming president of the Philippines.

Empowered by willing followers, she tapped into her leadership potential, translating personal crisis into decisive action. Similar stories can be told of Coretta Scott King who carries on the work of Martin

Luther King, Jr.; or Myrlie Evers-Williams, widow of slain civil rights leader Medgar Evers, who was recently elected as the first woman to chair the NAACP.

Mahatma Gandhi, a shy, humanist in his early life, was also propelled into exemplary leadership by his decisions following a critical turning point.

While en route to South Africa by train, he was denied access to a stage coach because of his race. He was so enraged by this injustice, that, in the words of B.R. Nanda, his biographer, "the iron entered his soul." At that point, he **resolved to change his world** by devoting his life to stamping out injustice.

To make the point of this chapter, I have chosen somewhat dramatic examples in which personal indignation or even rage may play a part in the individual's emergence into leadership. The simple lesson here is that leadership is tied to **conviction**. Leaders have a vision of a better future; they feel strongly about positively influencing the future. They reach inward and tap into their storehouse of experiences to empower, inspire, influence, and collaborate with others to successfully meet the future's challenges. A sense of purpose drives leaders; their actions are future-oriented and hopeful.

For some leaders, the moment of crisis that propels them forward is distinct and dramatic.

For others, like Margaret Thatcher, it is a steady evolution, in which the leader is groomed for success from birth. Thatcher was raised in a family active in community affairs, consumed with politics, religion, and the work ethic. Heavily influenced by her upbringing, Thatcher, upon entering Oxford University, immediately joined the Oxford University Conservative Association as a Tory. She became president of the Association in her senior year, and decided to pursue a career in politics upon graduation. By age 26, Thatcher won the Tory nomination representing the district of Dartford. This was quite a significant achievement at the time, especially since she was a "first": a young woman who defeated 26 other candidates, all male, for the political seat.

Thatcher's subsequent campaigns for political office were not all rosy. She was defeated twice in her attempt to be elected to Parliament. But her highly disciplined upbringing served her well. She campaigned with vigor, working day and night, and through this and other grueling ordeals, eventually earned the nickname, "The Iron Lady."

Her political career was firmly launched in 1959, when she won a seat in the House of Commons. By then she had married, attended law school and passed the bar exams (while five months pregnant with twins). While carrying out the traditional roles of wife, mother, and homemaker, she maintained her career with unrelenting vigor.

Margaret Thatcher's rise to Prime Minister of England in 1979 marked the culmination of years of struggle by a woman who was **groomed to succeed** by parental nurturing, academic and professional mentors, as well as the political climate in her country—in short, a total environment that called forth this woman's **innate leadership potential.**

It is easy to find documented examples of the lives and struggles of political, social, scientific, and artistic leaders and their journeys toward excellence. Other notables whose personal paths to leadership have been well documented include various members of the Kennedy family, General George Patton, educator Marva Collins, Winston Churchill, Golda Meir, Booker T. Washington, Mary McLeod Bethune, Albert Einstein, Madame Curie, Leonard Bernstein, Vincent Van Gogh, Pablo Picasso, and Paul Robeson, to name a few.

Only recently have we begun to document the lives of business people as the new "heroes." Biographies and autobiographies of H. Ross Perot, Lee Iacocca, Mary Kay Ash, and Oprah Winfrey now routinely make the bestseller lists, providing us with inspiring examples of the inner journey of those who choose to make their impact in business and industry.

Lee Iacocca, for example, admits to being an extremely shy person who balked at public presentations. In struggling with this personal challenge, he sought out Dale Carnegie courses and pushed himself to take on more and more challenging speaking engagements to improve his effectiveness. While I would not venture to attribute all of his corporate success to this single life crisis, his eventual mastery of media communications exemplifies the link between developmental struggles and resolving to lead.

Corporate leadership does not emanate only from management ranks, however. Anyone at any level in a company can exercise leadership. A Pittsburgh Paint and Glass (PPG) scientist recently demonstrated leadership when he saw an opportunity to turn waste into a viable product. He observed that the company's paint manufacturer customers generated a waste product that was expensive to dispose of. It occurred to the scientist that this waste could be reprocessed and sold as a low-grade paint to be applied to such products as industrial drums that did not require expensive applications. This technical research professional showed leadership as he championed this idea through all the proper internal channels. The customer now pays PPG less than it would to dispose of the product, for the service of retrieving and recycling the paint. The customer, and others, can then purchase the paint for other uses. In this clever, innovative move, everyone wins. By empowering a technical staff member, who is typically not charged with taking the company into new markets, PPG has created a motivating environment that supports the emergence of leadership in its employees.

When Mead D'Amore, general manager of Westinghouse's Commercial
Nuclear Fuel Division (CNFD), discusses his division's winning of the
first Malcolm Baldridge Quality Award in 1988, he mentions the words
"leadership," "culture change," and "employee ownership" frequently.
The Westinghouse model for Total Quality is based on the imperatives
of management leadership, product and process leadership, customer
orientation, and human resource excellence. D'Amore's preamble to his
"Leadership 2000" training program for managers and professionals
reads:

> At Westinghouse we recognize that excellence begins with leadership.
>
> Through exemplary leadership, we have developed and sustained our
> commitment to Total Quality in the way we do business.
>
> Through product and process leadership, we have distinguished
> ourselves in manufacturing, engineering, and management systems
> that allow us to meet and exceed customer expectations consistently.
>
> Through leadership in human resource management, we have
> involved, supported, and empowered our employees to be their very
> best, thereby reaping the rewards of excellence in the workplace.
>
> Through leadership that focuses on the customer's perception of value
> received from products and services, we have set world-class standards
> for being responsive and responsible in meeting our customers' needs.
>
> If we are to maintain and strengthen our position in the marketplace,
> we must continue to develop and empower our employees to exer-
> cise the quality leadership that has earned us distinction in the past.
> We must continue to instill an "ownership" culture in *all* of our
> employees . . .

This orientation to leadership throughout CNFD is echoed by Stephen
Deller, chairman of the Division Leadership Development Team, who,
in commenting on the division's transformation to a prize-winning
Total Quality culture, explained that the key ingredient for success

came from engaging every employee in the leadership processes by changing the expectations of management. According to Deller:

> What has happened, in simple terms, is that our managers changed their leadership styles, and our employees responded by changing their work styles. Today we're a different organization than we were several years ago. We work just as hard, but a good bit smarter, and we're having fun. Recognizing individual contributions through a variety of award programs and celebrating group accomplishments is now a way of life in the Division. We are experiencing leadership in action at *all levels* in the organization.

At a national Quality Award Conference, Division Manager Mead D'Amore captured the essence of employee leadership with the following insights, quoted in the September 1989 *Training & Development Journal:*

> People want to succeed. They want to do their best. They want to be their best. Create the right culture; give them the vision they can latch onto. Provide people the tools they need to get the job done. Show them you care about quality. Then get out of the way. Because great things will happen.

PART

THE
JOURNEY
INWARD

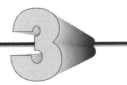

C H A P T E R

SELF-KNOWLEDGE: Prerequisite for Leadership

A basic premise of this book is that **even the greatest, most enabling leader is at the core an "ordinary person," with ordinary fears, concerns, and life challenges.** I take the somewhat irreverent position that all of us embody the potential to lead. Some of us tap this potential and use it to positively influence the situations in which we find ourselves. Others succumb to life pressures or are never challenged to exercise leadership. Still others harness it, but use it for self-serving or malevolent ends.

One thing is clear if we choose to lead. **To transform our organizations, our communities or our lives, we must first transform ourselves.** Leadership development, then, becomes a process of self-reflection aimed at personal growth: a journey inward.

Organizational renewal must begin with personal renewal because
organizations do not exist as entities apart from the people that
comprise them. *In fact, we re-create ourselves through our organizations.* If we are personally lacking in integrity, low in self-esteem,
or careless about our environment, then the organizations we create as
leaders will mirror our lack of values, our insecurities, or our careless-
ness. To create organizations or communities that are responsive and
responsible, we must first make sure that we are ourselves capable of
making the right decisions and acting with courage and responsibility.

Once we regularly engage in self-reflection, it becomes easier to be in
touch with the significance of the challenges and the opportunities
that present themselves in our personal and professional lives. We can
then consciously draw on and apply these lessons to the development
of a personal plan for our own leadership development.

When we are self-reflective and willing to explore the lessons behind
life crises, we tend to keep moving towards greater personal power
and influence. This means confronting each challenge, taking the atten-
dant risks, and developing new competence as a result. We adopt new
values when necessary and change directions as needed to create the
future we desire. This approach is often challenging. At times it evokes
deep-seated fears, because it requires that we lean into uncomfortable
situations and work through them in order to learn what possible
outcomes lurk behind the unknown. But for those who would make
an impact on their world, it is a path worth taking. In the words of
Marilyn Ferguson, author of the *Aquarian Conspiracy:*

> Risk always brings its own rewards: the exhilaration of breaking
> through, of getting to the other side; the relief of a conflict healed; the
> clarity when a paradox dissolves. Whoever teaches us, this is the agent
> of our liberation. Eventually we know deeply that the other side of
> every fear is freedom.

When we allow ourselves to become "stuck," we continue to experience life challenges or crises. At such times, however, we may put our energy into denying the significance of the challenges and their lessons. When we are "stuck," we avoid struggle or succumb to it. Sometimes we look for the easy way out. In the end, the very consequence we fear, such as loss of control or lack of power, becomes reality. As a result, we are not likely to exercise personal power, or leadership. Nor are we likely to attract followers, unless like tyrannical leaders possessed by fear and insecurity, we use manipulation or coercion to make others comply with our wishes. Thus, we must approach leadership and solve dilemmas with a greater sense of self, found through the journey inward.

Life Lessons

No two people are the same. Even identical twins have different footprints and unique elements of spirit. Similarly, each of us is given a life script that is ours alone. To become "unstuck," we must reflect on our lives and the lessons our experiences have taught us. This allows us to take stock of our strengths and weaknesses and redirect our energies appropriately. In the discussion that follows, you will be given an opportunity to chart your lifeline and reflect on your personal lessons of leadership so far.

Each of us has a special combination of strengths and weaknesses, trials and successes, that is like no other. The effective leader learns to accept his or her own individuality and the individuality of others. We are each given a unique set of experiences and beliefs that shape who we are and what we bring to the acts of leadership we perform. At the same time, the leader is able to help harness these differences to build high-performing teams. This is carried out in much the same way that a conductor leads a symphony to produce beautiful music, by combining the input of different players with their individual instruments and skill levels.

Our lives unfold as a series of stories told to us by the events and people we encounter, and by the results of the choices we make along the way. Each story brings a special message. Each holds a lesson to be learned as we develop wisdom and strategies of recreating the situations we want. Often we ignore these lessons. As a result, we repeat them over and over until we become enlightened. This is why if you review your life stories, you will notice certain recurring themes or patterns. For example, you may find that each time you are on the verge of financial success something occurs to set you back. Or you may find that you are attracted, over and over again, to a certain kind of relationship that starts in a particular way and ends in a particular way.

Life mapping is a process that allows you to identify your own patterns —both ineffective and effective—by creating a life lesson chart. By becoming aware of your patterns, you can redirect your energy and create more positive outcomes for yourself. You can do this in two ways:

1. You can identify patterns that block your success, then "re-program" these negative patterns by consciously changing your behavioral choices.

2. You can identify patterns that have created your successes, then consciously make behavioral choices that reinforce and build upon these positive patterns.

I offer this excerpt from my own life story as an example:

> At the very early age of three, I was given a minor role in a concert at the elementary school where my mother taught. I was to mount

the seemingly vast stage and recite a poem that went simply: "Look, there's a spider on the wall. That's all!"

Filled with anticipation, I was hoisted up on to the stage by my mother, and in what was to become my earliest recollection of consciousness, I thought: "I don't see a spider. I won't say those words!" So I stood there transfixed, saying nothing as all the teachers, sitting in the front row of the auditorium, whispered in increasingly nervous tones, "Go ahead, honey, say the poem. Go ahead. . . 'Look there's a spider . . .' Go ahead. Don't be scared!"

To which I finally replied defiantly: "I won't say it. There is no spider on the wall!"

So they put the concert on hold, scurried around, drew a huge spider on black construction paper and glued it to the wall. At which point, filled with satisfaction that I could now act with integrity by telling the truth, I pointed proudly to the spider I helped to create, and with a grand, dramatic flourish intoned loudly: "Look, there's a spider on the wall. That's all!"

I can still recall the feeling of power and accomplishment, as parents chuckled with delight and the audience applauded. I think I decided then and there that school was a great place, and I liked the feeling of having a positive impact on a group of people.

By the age of three-and-a-half, I became annoyed that the adults around me could read and I couldn't. They read newspapers and street signs and bedtime stories to me. I listened, but could only decipher the pictures and not the words in the books. So I decided to embrace books. In fact, I carried the first grade primer my mother gave me everywhere I went. And I implored her always to teach me to read. She gladly accommodated me.

At that point I once again became impatient. I wasn't yet enrolled in school, even though I could read (and write). My cousins went to school; why couldn't I? So my mother used her influence to get the headmistress at her school to make an exception and enroll me in kindergarten class at age three, instead of four. I organized a group of children in my class, and spent all my free time conducting my own school-within-a-school teaching these children everything I knew.

These early childhood accomplishments were rewarded and nurtured by proud parents who regularly paraded me in front of guests to recite poetry or participate in "adult" discussions about politics and my own budding brand of philosophy. High achievement both academically and in sports seemed to come effortlessly over the next decade of my life and I enjoyed great popularity as a member of the debate team and a host of other extracurricular activities.

Then at age fifteen, the bottom fell out of my world.

My family migrated to New York City, and I had to start all over in a strange, new culture; lifelong friends left behind; feeling too self-conscious about my foreign accent to join the debate team or speak in front of a group; having my self-esteem seriously challenged for the first time since my stage debut at age three. I struggled for two years to regain my equilibrium, I immersed myself in the one area that I knew held positive rewards: academic excellence. I buried myself in books and school-related activities, including the risky business of joining the debate team in spite of my trepidation about my "difference." I was elected class president in my senior year of high school in this strange new culture, and graduated with flying colors, the idea of teaching for a living etched indelibly in my psyche.

The above are highlights of some of my "life leadership lessons" from the first seventeen years of my life. If I were to map my "spider on the wall" life lesson on a chart, it would look like the summary that follows.

AGE 0–10

Critical Life Events
Stage debut at age three.

Feelings
Anxiety followed by the
thrill of achievement.

Key Persons
Mother, teachers

Impact
Made me feel empowered;
built my self-esteem.

Critical Personal Choices
My decision to perform.

Results
I view group performance
and teaching as positive.

Even today, the "spider" lesson influences my life, in the career I've chosen, for example. When teaching, I often reconnect with the "stage" experience of my childhood, especially when others respond positively to my message. When I act with conviction or take a risk I often recall the little girl on stage and become centered in her power.

Now I invite you to chart your own life lessons, and discover the lessons for yourself. You can be as detailed as you would like to be. Invite someone close to you to participate in the exercise, if you wish. Then you can take turns talking about your life lessons: the highs, the lows, and the lessons learned or strengths discovered in each case. Map your life lessons in the charts on pages 32–41.

AGE 1-10

Critical Life Events   **Feelings**

Key Persons   **Impact**

Critical Personal Choices   **Results**

AGE 11-15

Critical Life Events

Feelings

Key Persons

Impact

Critical Personal Choices

Results

AGE 16-25

Critical Life Events   **Feelings**

Key Persons   **Impact**

Critical Personal Choices   **Results**

AGE 26-35

Critical Life Events   **Feelings**

Key Persons   **Impact**

Critical Personal Choices   **Results**

AGE 36-45

Critical Life Events   **Feelings**

Key Persons   **Impact**

Critical Personal Choices   **Results**

AGE 46–55

Critical Life Events   **Feelings**

Key Persons   **Impact**

Critical Personal Choices   **Results**

AGE 56-65

Critical Life Events   **Feelings**

Key Persons   **Impact**

Critical Personal Choices   **Results**

AGE 66-75

Critical Life Events   **Feelings**

Key Persons   **Impact**

Critical Personal Choices   **Results**

AGE 76–85

Critical Life Events   **Feelings**

Key Persons   **Impact**

Critical Personal Choices   **Results**

AGE 86–100

Critical Life Events   **Feelings**

Key Persons   **Impact**

Critical Personal Choices   **Results**

Now, it's time to take stock of where you've been and where you currently are in your personal and professional life. Review your life lessons with the questions provided below, and as I continue to reveal aspects of the leadership journey throughout the book, you may want to refer back to your life lessons chart.

1. **What themes do you notice about your life lessons?**

2. **What personal strengths seem apparent?**

3. **What would you like to celebrate about your life?**

4. **Now go back to the life lessons chart and project into the future from your present age to age 100. What critical events and lessons do you anticipate? Use your imagination and create your future.**

Leadership, Followership and Motivation

————————————— Scholarly attempts to define leadership vary widely. People who attempt to define leadership do so according to their own perspectives or their own personal experiences. It is very much like the definition of the elephant as perceived by the blind men in Aesop's fable. Each described the part of the animal that he stood near and could touch. One described the shape and size of the tail, another a leg, and so on; all different but true. Combine the descriptions, and they make up the whole animal.

Here, then, is an attempt to piece together an understanding of leadership, followership, and motivation based on contemporary writers' perceptions.

John Gardner, founding chairman of the think tank Common Cause and a exemplary leader in his own right, now devotes his time to the study of leadership. In the first of several papers on leadership he defines it as "the process of persuasion and example by which an individual (or leadership team) induces a group to take action that is in accord with the leader's purposes or the shared purposes of all."

A leader, says Gardner in subsequent papers, cannot be viewed separately from followers. Followers, by their consent to follow, call forth the leader. **One rises to leadership, and continues to lead only so long as followers empower one to do so.** This claim holds the key to "motivation," for it suggests that a leader induces commitment from followers if the leader clearly demonstrates his or her willingness to help followers meet their needs.

Writing about the power of the follower in today's "new workforce," Robert Kelley says in his book, *The Gold Collar Worker,* that new work ethics—"risk-taking, tolerance, mutual respect, responsible participation, interdependence, balance between professional and extracurricular pursuits, and a high quality of life"—guide the expectations of many professionals. He goes on to add: "They want a good job but are less driven by the external rewards of promotion and status. They are not innocently attracted to power, nor do they want to follow." This interesting perspective would challenge our assumptions about traditional leadership.

Peter Drucker, a seasoned management consultant, takes yet another approach to explaining leadership and how leaders emerge. In a 1988 *Wall Street Journal* article on leadership, Drucker concludes that leadership has little to do with special qualities such as charisma; it is simply performance. Says Drucker: "More doing than dash." By this definition, the person who perceives an opportunity or fills a need emerges as a leader, provided he or she meets the expectations of followers.

Influenced by James MacGregor Burns' work on leadership in the late 1970s, Warren Bennis and Burt Nanus explore the concept of "transformative leadership" in their book, *Leaders*. They describe this contemporary version of the leader as "one who commits people to action, who converts followers into leaders, and who may convert leaders into agents of change." In the final chapter of their book, Bennis and Nanus talk about the "symbiotic relationship between leaders and followers," and suggest that for transformative leadership to occur the leader must "reflect the community of interests of both leaders and followers."

They then go on to make the now often quoted distinction between managing and leading: "Managers are people who do things right, and leaders are people who do the right thing. The difference may be summarized as activities of vision and judgment—effectiveness—versus activities of mastering routines—efficiency."

Leadership and Followership

After reviewing the more recent writings on leadership, I chose to include only those definitions that acknowledge or imply that leadership and followership are opposite sides of the same coin. Scholars who attempt to define leadership without discussing followership have missed a key point: **You can "lead" all you want, but if you look around you and there is no one following, you are not exercising leadership**. Furthermore, you can only lead for as long as followers permit you to—for as long as they see you as a credible and trustworthy source of influence. A "follower," as the term is used throughout this book, needn't be subordinate in an organizational sense to the leader. A follower is anyone who feels empowered by the leader's vision and example, and who is therefore committed to working jointly toward shared goals. At times the followers may be your boss, the board of directors, your children, constituents whom you affect positively through your lobbying efforts, or your employees.

Management, leadership, and followership are, of course, all situational. At times the effective leader must put all of his or her energies into managing. That's what it takes to **implement and secure the vision**. At times the leader must step out in front of the pack, taking risks and championing new causes. At other times, *the leader must follow*. In fact, **the best leaders are good followers**. They seek input; they ask for help; they are able to modify their position when they discover that their choices are ill-advised. They are able to give away power, and in so doing invite their followers to participate in shared leadership— a pooling of everyone's talents towards the common goal.

In his article "In Praise of Followers," Robert Kelley lists four qualities of effective followers. Interestingly, these qualities epitomize leadership as well:

1. They manage themselves well.

2. They commit to the organization and to a purpose, principle, or person outside themselves.

3. They build their competence and focus their efforts for maximum impact.

4. They are courageous, honest, and credible.

Kelley further asserts: "Instead of seeing the leadership role as superior to and more active than the role of the follower, we can think of them as equal but different activities."

Leadership is ultimately measured by the leader's impact on lives—his or her own as well as others', and as suggested throughout this book, **the best results occur when leaders create a "motivating envi-**

ronment." In Chapter 2, I raised the question: "Why do some people choose to lead while others follow, or still others do neither?" In other words, what **motivates** people to take action? We have all heard incredible stories of people who perform superhuman feats in a crisis. A *Time Magazine* article several years ago reported the story of a frail, ailing mother, who lifted a 3,300-pound station wagon to release her son, who was pinned beneath it. Barbara Grogan, founder of Western Industrial Contractors, a six million dollar a year millwrighting firm in Denver, is an interesting example of how motivation can spark impressive action. At age thirty-five, faced with the crisis of divorce, she transformed her life from that of an insecure woman to a wealthy entrepreneur. Armed with a psychology degree, very little money, and even less experience, she chose to start a contracting business because she thought no one would hire her. Since contracting allowed her to lease equipment and sub-contract business on a project-by-project basis, it required very little start-up capital. So she plunged in, paradoxically motivated by fear and the need to feed her children.

When we observe the behavior of people in crisis who choose to take control of the situation, the definition of motivation becomes clearer. **The first component of the motivated person's behavior has to do with focus.** Given the alternatives of action versus inertia, he or she **focuses on action**. The second component relates to effort: the motivated person's **behavior is powerful and persistent. A motivated person directs his or her behavior towards some desired outcome in a focused and persistent way.** While leaders tend to be highly motivated, fewer than 25 percent of today's workers claim that they work to their full potential, according to a 1983 study by Daniel Yankelovich. I believe that this is due in part to poor leadership. Today's organizations have consistently created a "demotivating" environment by discouraging risk-taking, failing to include those who are "different," and taking the creativity, challenge, and fun out of work for the masses.

As the impact of technology, global economic crises, demographic shifts, and changing human values create constant change in our communities and organizations, the need for a motivating environment becomes more pressing every day. We need leaders who can help people to become aligned and energized to make the right decisions and move in the right direction.

Personal Leadership and Motivation

Motivation is related to leadership on two levels: **personal leadership** and **group leadership**. On the personal level, leaders at their best are **focused** and **persistent**. Their energies are directed. They find personal satisfaction and even joy in what they are pursuing. They become single-minded about the cause or the goal they are supporting. They then unleash all their thoughts, emotions, and talents in the desired direction. As they persistently move forward in this state of mind, distractions, disappointments, or setbacks are seen as problems to be solved or as lessons to be learned in order to improve performance. They then continue toward their goal with renewed resolve and heightened awareness.

Most of the trainees who participate in my leadership seminars are chosen by their organizations because of their demonstrated managerial and professional skills and their dedication to leadership goals. The course is part of their career development strategy. It is not unusual for these trainees to comment that they are having so much fun, or enjoying the challenge of the work so much that their salary is a "bonus" to the real payoffs of the job. Liver transplant pioneer, Dr. Thomas Starzl, in discussing his own unswerving motivational level during a recent NBC news interview, put it this way: "Some people get burnout. Other people only get a stronger desire to make things better. I hope I fit into that category."

Starzl is credited with performing more organ transplants than any other surgeon. He accomplished this by taking heroic risks, often putting his entire medical career at stake as he took risks with new procedures or new drugs in his all-consuming attempt to "make things better." Starzl's love of medicine was initially inspired by his mother, a nurse in the small Iowa town where he grew up. His extraordinary vision and persistence are linked to personal character traits that drive him to seek out challenging situations for the sheer thrill of doing something others thought impossible. In fact, he admits he chose his work in medicine specifically with the liver because it is the largest glandular organ—and the most complex.

This intense personal motivation allows Thomas Starzl to persist amidst repeated setbacks, pessimism and condemnation from medical colleagues at different points in his exemplary career. His latest success involves FK-506, a new immunosuppressant administered to transplant patients to reduce the risk of organ rejection. Again, he pioneered this controversial new treatment amid demands that would diminish the motivation of the bravest souls, and yet he persisted in spite of his own health problems. With his surgical procedures for organ transplantation firmly established in the medical community, Starzl recently turned his attention to different research challenges at his newly established Transplant Institute.

Group Leadership and Motivation

The study of motivation theory helps us to understand that motivation is **not** something that a leader **does to** followers. There are two bodies of research on motivation. Both support the same kind of conclusions about what motivates people. The "content theorists" tell us that specific factors such as human needs for safety, inclusion, self-esteem, or personal fulfillment motivate us. "Process theorists" tell us that motivation comes from two human dynamics: we receive positive or negative reinforcement (internally or from others) for our actions, or we believe we will be rewarded or punished for those actions. The path and behaviors we choose in a given situation are tied to our perception of the likely outcome.

While it is possible for the leader to use reinforcement (reward and punishment) to modify group members' behaviors so they fulfill organizational goals, this is not "motivation" in the sense being discussed here. In fact, in many instances such attempts at "motivation" may be experienced as coercion or manipulation by group members. This is especially true when the rewards are not tied to individual members' expressed **needs**. However, a leader can "motivate" a group by creating a climate that supports individual initiative and ownership in the group's process. In such a climate motivation works best because it is generated intrinsically (internally by the follower).

When Ralph Dickerson took on the leadership of the United Way of New York City, he was appalled to learn that 45 percent of African American and 60 percent of Hispanic American students drop out between middle school and high school. Recognizing that schools are being given the unreasonable task of "being everything to everyone," and that students arrive with multiple problems beyond the scope of teachers, Dickerson and his leadership team decided to offer a challenge to the Board of Education to do some things differently. The challenge? To get community-based organizations to work with the schools. Create entrepreneurial opportunities for community groups to serve the schools in their own neighborhoods. This would facilitate the process of education on an ongoing basis, both in and out of school.

The joint Board of Education/United Way Advisory Team formed as a result of this vision, motivated the Board of Education to grant forty million dollars over three years for a project that currently involves eighty schools in the city's toughest neighborhoods, and fifty-four community-based organizations, spawning one hundred nineteen different programs and affecting ten thousand to twelve thousand children and their families. Says Dickerson, "We were able to achieve this by simply laying out a course of action, **taking time to listen** to the Board of Education, the children themselves, the children's families, and the community agencies. We brought these groups together, but it is working because it is driven by their needs and their input."

Richard Nicolosi is often cited as an industry leader whose focus on creating the right business environment motivated employees to transform a declining market into impressive profits against major competition. Nicolosi was promoted to Proctor & Gamble's Paper Products division at a time when the division's market share for disposable diapers was declining rapidly. Undaunted by slipping profits, he immediately set about empowering all employees to become leaders in their own right. They were supported in developing a team approach in which they were given responsibility well beyond what was typical for the formerly hierarchical bureaucracy Nicolosi inherited. As Nicolosi and his leadership team flattened layer after layer in his organization's hierarchy, they encouraged workers to "shun the incremental and go for the leap." As reported in May–June 1990 *Harvard Business Review* article "What Leaders Really Do," the outcome of Nicolosi's vision and leadership acumen was as follows:

> . . . large numbers of people were motivated to realize the new vision. Most, introduced in February 1985, took the market share of the entire Pampers product line from 40 percent to 58 percent and profitability from break-even to positive. And within only a few months of the introduction of Luvs Deluxe in May 1987, market share for the overall brand grew by 150 percent.

> . . . In the spring of 1986, a few of the division's secretaries, feeling empowered by the new culture, developed a Secretaries Network.

This association established subcommittees on training, on reward and recognition, and on the "secretary of the future." Echoing the sentiments of many of her peers, one paper products secretary said: "I don't see why we too can't contribute to the division's new direction."

On the group leadership level, then, leaders at their best **create a motivating environment**. They do so by empowering group members to find ways to align their self-interests with organizational goals. As demonstrated throughout this book, each individual has a unique set of experiences, and therefore different personal needs and values. Leaders who understand this respond to group members as individuals, each with his or her own special perspective, each capable of being **focused** and persistent in his or her own important way.

The Leader's Character

Contrary to what popular management theory may have led us to believe, there is **no right style of leadership for today's world.** As social style profiling of leaders from all walks of life has shown, leaders influence people using a variety of styles. Some leaders achieve great outcomes using a style that is task-oriented and intensely driven. Others are quiet, reflective, and low-keyed in they way they relate to people. Some are creative and unique, challenging the process and interrelating in ways no one has encountered before—they may be labeled mavericks, and even "crazy," but are still effective using this style. The quiet, yet shrewd visionary Mahatma Gandhi, was an impressive leader; so was the colorful, yet strategic General MacArthur. The warm, self-sacrificial Mother Teresa is a powerful leader; so is the dignified, persistent Shirley Chisholm.

In my work as a management consultant, I often encounter managers who ask me to help them change their **style** of managing; some even speak of finding ways to emulate an outstanding leader they know. The point they often miss is that if they contrive a new style that is inconsistent with their personality, followers have an uncanny ability to detect such behavior as being inauthentic. This will eventually erode trust—a prerequisite for a mutually satisfying work relationship.

The point of this chapter is this: **character is more important than style** in determining leadership effectiveness. Accordingly to Piaget and other developmental theorists, your style or personality is relatively fixed. It developed at an early age and will likely remain the same over your lifetime. What you can, and should, change as you become a more effective human being is your *versatility*. Effective leaders often leave the comfort of their "home-base" style, and use a variety of approaches in interacting with others. So while your personality may have you feeling most comfortable when focused intensely on a task, to the exclusion of other people, you may need to develop and use good interpersonal skills to build relationships and trust as you lead. Conversely, if your style is innately "people-oriented," to be an effective leader you may need to be task-oriented when the situation calls for that.

Character on the other hand, has to do with leadership traits. Regardless of your style, are you honest or dishonest? Do your espoused values match your actions? Do you demonstrate courage? Are your actions guided by concern for others? Are you trustworthy? These are the questions of character that followers ask. These are the traits they seek in leaders.

To be an effective leader you must be **trustworthy**. To engage followers and create change in yourself and others you must consistently demonstrate that:

1. You are honest (tell your truth heroically or admit when you don't know).

2. You **do** what you **say** you believe in, and you do it consistently.

3. You have your followers' best interests at heart: **you care**.

4. You can **act with conviction** (take a strong stand), and you can **listen and follow** (learn from others or admit when you're wrong).

If your followers (employees, colleagues, customers, family members, friends, constituents) believe these things to be true **as demonstrated by your behavior**, you will very credibly exercise leadership, simply by "being." To achieve this requires self-reflection and spiritual development, as well as demonstrated competence. The path is challenging, yet rewarding. First examine the motives that drive your behaviors. Look at the feelings and attitudes you have about your work, your community, and your family to make sure you are in the right place, doing the right things. Then find out what your gifts are, and embrace and develop these fully. Finally, discern your followers' needs and motives, and be responsible and responsive in acting on what you learn. Wise leaders listen to what followers seek. With impressive regularity, workers in every sector I have consulted list similar expectations of leaders:

1. **Followers want congruence between your "rhetoric" and your behavior.** In my work with organizations involved in planned change, one of the most demoralizing behaviors (based on employee complaints) is the failure of management to lead by example. "Walk the talk" is now a popular adage touted by disappointed followers who observe would-be leaders listing lofty ideals in their mission statements, while behaving in ways that are contradictory to those values. The net result is a loss of trust that impedes management's ability to engage followers.

2. **Followers want authentic caring, not manipulation or showmanship.** Leaders in all sectors often go after the right

changes for the wrong reasons. Often I encounter clients who say: "We need to be less autocratic and promote more employee involvement because then they won't resist the changes we have planned." While involving employees in decisions that will affect them is the right thing to do **most** of the time, it is often done for the wrong reasons. We should involve employees because it honors who they are and what they bring to bear on solving business problems. It is both the right thing and the smart thing to do, from a business perspective. **But if it is done simply as a manipulative ploy to avoid employee resistance, it will be perceived as such.** If, for example, the manager calls a meeting to ask for input, after having already made the decision (as is often done in organizations), the lack of trust that this engenders is more devastating than if the manager exercised true leadership: a willingness to tell the truth, in this case that a command decision has been made. The leader's and the followers' needs would be better served by admitting that a top-down decision was made. I am convinced that workers would rather be told: "We're doing this because we see it as the only way out," or "Management made this decision under the constraints of our regulators, and it is not negotiable," rather than "We're doing this for your own good," or "Give us your ideas,"—after the fact.

3. **Followers want their needs and values to count.** If a leader fails to know his or her followers, the leader loses momentum and fails—unless the followers become convinced that present values and beliefs no longer serve them. This is in fact the greatest leadership challenge for those who undertake major culture change in any organization, even when invited to do so by would-be followers. This is where patience, persistence, competence, and the ability to inspire and lead by example,

become critical for both leader and followers. If the leader consistently fails to help followers achieve desired results or denies followers their rights and expectations, they will eventually become disillusioned and will remove the leader either by "brute force" or more often, by non-compliance and lack of commitment. The leader is empowered only so long as he or she understands the followers' needs and motivations.

It is also important to know your followers because, as explained in Chapter 1, followers and leaders are inextricably linked. Honest, ethical, concerned followers demand these qualities in their leaders. Conversely, followers who are dishonest or unethical can reinforce or call forth these behaviors in their leaders.

4. **Followers need power—the capacity to ensure the outcomes they want.** That's why they seek leaders in the first place! Shared leadership is most effective. Yet, this does not mean that the leader cannot act with conviction. At times the leader may be convinced that his or her personal vision holds the best solution for the future. At those times the leader may, through persuasion and example, attempt to negotiate a strong coalition or support for the vision. This is not the same as manipulation or coercion, **if the motivation is in the best interests of the followers**. In fact, in many instances, followers seek this "conviction" in a leader. They may ask for clarity of direction, or "strong leadership." At other times, however, the goals of followers should be allowed to supersede the leader's personal vision or at least to modify it. Thus, the leader must be flexible and responsive. The effective leader must know how to listen and integrate the needs of followers. Remember, "ownership" is at the heart of a motivated work team.

In developing our character as leaders, our inner journey may require us to take "the road less travelled." Consider the following pathways.

From Anger to Forgiveness

Psychologists tell us that "anger turned inward" can lead to depression, guilt feelings, or feelings of inadequacy. Obviously this state of mind clouds our vision and causes inertia. As the philosopher Montaigne put it, "There is no passion that so shakes the clarity of our judgment as anger." If we mismanage anger by directing it inward or misdirecting it at the wrong persons, we create conditions that will make us less effective human beings. Anger directed at ourselves can cause us to procrastinate, make poor decisions, or engage in compulsive behaviors that can become barriers to personal and professional success. Anger aimed at others—family members, coworkers, racial or ethnic groups, and so forth—can damage important relationships or impede our ability to act fairly and humanely.

When we choose to lead, we are concerned with such behaviors as involving and supporting others, creating a motivating environment to achieve goals, setting a clear, ennobling vision, and attracting others to that vision. If, for example, the would-be leader is preoccupied by anger with his or her parents for mistakes they made, or angry with historical wrongs committed against his or her ethnic group, or angry with "the system" in which the person works, it is less likely that he or she will be able to respond effectively to the interpersonal demands of leadership.

This does not mean that leaders do not or should not experience anger. Anger often signals us that something is wrong; that something needs to change. Feeling angry may alert us that our basic needs or values are being affronted. The anxiety caused by anger can lead us to take positive steps to relieve our discomfort and return us to a more contented state. In such cases, anger becomes a catalyst for change—an opportunity to exercise leadership by confronting and working through the circumstances that incited our anger. It does mean, however, that to succeed the leader must learn to express anger appropriately, then **LET IT GO** in order to focus positively on the work ahead. By working through and releasing our anger, we free ourselves emotionally to address the cause of the anger by demonstrating positive, constructive leadership.

In my life's work, I am acutely aware of the racial inequities in the upper ranks of corporate America. As I conduct leadership training seminars, I am reminded daily that so-called "minorities" (African Americans, Hispanics, Native Americans, Asians) and women are practically missing from key decision-making positions in business. My awareness is compounded in a very personal way by some of the mistaken assumptions people make about me based on my race and gender. These personal reminders, innocent though they may be on the part of the individuals involved, sometimes trigger my anger.

To remain positive, effective, and caring as a human resource professional, I must daily find ways to work past my anger, let it go, and view my position as an opportunity to make a positive impact on a less-than-perfect world. Through my personal experiences I have learned that anger can become a positive force in leadership development if the following mindset prevails.

1. **Diagnose and acknowledge personal feelings of anger**. People who are afraid of "losing control" often deny their anger. The result is often indulgence in passive aggressive behaviors, which in the long run tend to be more destructive than healthy expressed anger. Where appropriate, this includes being able to verbalize, "This makes me angry because . . ."

2. **Understand that not every battle is worth fighting**. The short-term gains of "being right" are often not worth the long-term costs. As Carol Tavris puts it in her book, *Anger*, "Sometime the best thing you can do about anger is nothing at all. Let it go, and half the time it will turn out to be an unimportant, momentary shudder, quickly forgotten."

3. **View anger as a potential motivator for positive change**. I know a highly successful research chemist who chose to become a leader in his field largely because of an incident that made him angry. His high school chemistry teacher insensitively told him that he showed no aptitude in the subject and should avoid taking any more chemistry courses. He chose the following thought pattern: "If I apply myself, surely I can master chemistry." As a result his **feelings** were those of being challenged, rather than discouraged. The **action** he then chose was to throw himself into a pursuit of the subject, and in the process developed both a great love for and expertise in it.

4. **Know when and how to use anger strategically** to draw attention to critical issues, then release it in order to address those issues with a clear head. When individuals march in protest, they draw attention to injustices that upset them. To address an agenda for change with those who are the source of their anger, the leadership must then move past the anger in order to direct their energies toward solutions.

5. **Develop the ability to forgive others**. People who harbor long-term grudges do great damage to their own psyches. At the same time they become less effective as leaders. A leader who is consciously or unconsciously motivated by residual anger, not only impairs his or her own judgment, but is less able to inspire and motivate others to take positive steps for change. When I

meet employees who are unable to work past their anger about their unmet needs in the workplace, I often observe a distortion in the way they interpret even the most "innocent" decision or action of their superiors. If your goal is to hone your leadership skills, it is important to remember the impact of residual anger on our ability to interpret events accurately and make **sound** decisions.

This brings us to a second, important pathway.

From "Nibbling" to Empowerment

People who feel powerless are less capable of empowering others. They horde information and are less apt to encourage others to fully develop. Leaders at their best share power; they find ways to allow their followers to share the responsibility for creating conditions that are best for the followers and for those whose goals and interests are at stake.

Bob Carpenter, a sales manager in a major electronics firm, is a typical example of how less powerful people operate. Three years ago he hired a new sales representative who turned out to be an exceptionally impressive employee. Not only was Bob's new hire well-liked by customers and employees, she routinely broke sales records in her department. Bob's boss noticed, as did everyone else, and he recommended that Bob begin to "groom Barb for a management position."

When I met Barbara Jones, the new sales rep, she had sought me out for counseling because she felt that no matter what she did, her boss, Bob Carpenter, failed to support her. He never acknowledged her excellent performance, withheld key information needed in her job, and began to avoid interacting with her whenever he could.

Because I was employed as a consultant at Bob and Barbara's firm, I had access to input from Bob, Barbara, and several other people who observed this scenario. When I spoke with Bob about his working relationship with Barbara, he said she was "too aggressive" and "power hungry." When I spoke with Bob's colleagues, several insisted that Bob had always felt insecure about his current position and had a history of ignoring the most successful members of his sales force. In fact, he typically devoted most of his time to those who were struggling and less likely to vie for management positions.

Three years later, disillusioned with her experience under Bob's management, Barbara left to join a competitor's firm. She now reported to Donald Butler, another client of mine. I casually asked Donald how Barbara was doing in her new job. His response was "I think I have found my potential replacement!" he then went on to discuss with great enthusiasm his plans for coaching and grooming Barbara for management. At the end of his conversation with me, he added: "You know I'm developing a real knack for finding good people."

This experience reinforced what I have repeatedly observed about leadership and power: **people who feel powerless may try to minimize the potential of others so they can feel more powerful by comparison**.

Kaleel Jamison, in her book, *The Nibble Theory,* wrote: "Many people look at themselves and they look at others and they think that the way to get bigger themselves is to get others down to size, make others smaller. So they start to nibble."

Nibbling takes many forms. It may involve withholding information from others so they are less capable of making sound decisions. Often this kind of nibbling can be seen in the behavior of people experiencing major organizational change. Department X may withhold information from Department Y to protect their power base or turf. Managers may withhold information from subordinates to keep them "subordinated."

When faced with the challenges of organizational change, the effective leader involves subordinates by sharing information freely, thereby **empowering** them to act from an **informed** position. Such an approach engenders creativity and, in the long run, facilitates the transition process.

Another way that people nibble others down to size is to offer only criticism about poor performance while refusing to acknowledge successes. This approach to leadership erodes self-esteem and diminishes the likelihood of sustained high performance.

To tap our leadership potential we must move from nibbling to empowerment. By inviting people to be their best, we nurture personal power and excellence in ourselves and others.

The third pathway holds the key to survival in our emerging global economy, marked by unprecedented uncertainty and dynamism.

From Rigidity to Flexibility

Processionary caterpillars travel in long lines, one behind the other, following their leader for great distances in search of food. Jean-Henri Fabre, a French naturalist, once conducted an interesting experiment with these caterpillars. He enticed the leader onto the rim of a large flowerpot. As the followers crowded onto the rim, the leader found himself head-to-tail with the last caterpillar, in a closed circle.

Locked into their instinctive behavior, the caterpillars circled the rim for seven days until each died of hunger and exhaustion, even though there was a large, visible supply of food nearby! The caterpillars' inability to break out of the habit led to their extinction.

Transforming communities, organizations, or ourselves is much like sailing the high seas. You set your sights on the land ahead, but must continually correct your course as you get blown off track. Success usually comes as a result of having a vision of where you would like to go or how you would like your life to be. You must then be able to focus on that vision whether or not your finances permit it, or your parents condone it, or your other commitments compete with it. Paradoxically enough, while our vision remains fixed, our actions must be flexible.

Inflexible entities soon become obsolete. Successful organizations continually change their practices, services, and product lines to adapt to changing customer values, competition, new technologies and employee needs. Individuals are the same way. In his book, *Transitions,* William Bridges suggests that our lives are marked by a series of transitions. Our childhood conditioning about how to deal with endings will determine to a large extent how we handle the disorientation, fear, and disenchantment that accompany change.

If we are to become more effective in leading others, we must first develop sound, healthy practices for managing our personal change. As Bridges points out: "In the transition process, we come to beginnings only at the end. It is when the endings and the time of fallow neutrality are finished that we can launch ourselves out anew, changed and renewed by the destruction of the old life-phase."

In addition to being comfortable with personal change, the wise leader must also be sensitive to the impact of change on group dynamics or organizational behavior. It is important to be aware of the following predictable patterns that complicate the change process, preventing people from "letting go" and moving forward.

1. **Everyone, including those who proposed or implemented the change, experiences "loss."** This may be manifested as disorientation, loss of identity, loss of security, uncertainty, or disenchantment. They may feel ambivalence about the future as they move from what was "known" and comfortable, to what is "unknown" and therefore less comfortable.

2. **Change is typically accompanied by a temporary decline in productivity and an increase in anxiety.** This is due to a variety of factors. First, the sense of loss described above is accompanied by a grieving process that may immobilize those involved as they deal with denial, anger or confusion. Second, change usually requires learning new skills, using new approaches, and building new relationships. This takes time. It also means that for a while participants in the process become less competent than they were under old, familiar conditions. Even the most experienced member of the transition group must deal with feeling "inexperienced" again. Finally, change usually results in more work until (new) order is firmly implemented. This can become a major reason for resistance, especially in organizations where employees felt overworked or understaffed prior to initiation of the change.

3. **Communication disruptions tend to accompany change.** Sometimes the breakdown in communication is due to poor planning or lack of trust. At other times it is due to the necessary restructuring of roles, relations, and expectations. Communication problems during change can also be linked to the absence of adequate information or skills.

The following attitudes and behaviors typically occur when leaders manage change well:

◆ **Leaders recognize that every change represents a loss of what was familiar and allow themselves and others time to mourn that loss.** They discuss their feelings about the necessary transition openly and encourage others involved to do the same.

◆ **Leaders look for ways to help everyone—including themselves—regain a sense of control.** This may be accomplished by sharing information and involving people in decisions that will affect them.

◆ **Leaders are clear about the direction in which they want to move** and delineate specific goals and expectations in a way that captures the imagination of others.

◆ **Leaders mobilize followers by providing resources,** or creating an environment that encourages followers to be creative about finding resources to facilitate the movement toward goals. Instinctively or by experience, leaders recognize the importance of deploying **time, money, talents, skills, and technology** to the process of change.

◆ **Leaders give top priority to communication.** They clarify their vision repeatedly, using a variety of media. They share information fully and in a timely fashion. They recognize that communication is a two-way street, so they **listen** to messages accordingly.

The fourth pathway involves new choices in *how* we engage others.

From Manipulation to Authenticity

Workplace values are undergoing a dramatic shift that I believe will pave the way for the kind of personal leadership that this book addresses. We are experiencing a shift from what Peter Drucker describes in *The Empowered Manager* as "myopic self-interest" to "enlightened self-interest." According to Drucker, the patriarchal values of the traditional workplace reinforce our instincts toward upward mobility by emphasizing control and authority as the primary measures of success. Conversely, new workplace norms are beginning to encourage employees to redefine success. Increasingly, the focus today is on service to external and internal customers. Employees want work that has meaning for them personally, that allows them to contribute to business goals through individual initiative, and, while monetary rewards are still important, they also want to integrate all facets of their life—work, play, relationships, and so forth. In keeping with these trends, the new workplace is also beginning to create opportunities for people to be more authentic, vocal, and candid. Personal effectiveness and leadership are now linked to the following behaviors:

1. **Using "straight-talk"**—being willing to say what we truly think.

2. **Challenging the status quo**—being willing to take the risk of questioning old practices or suggesting new ones when appropriate.

3. **Showing integrity**—being clear about what we value and making sure that our actions are consistent with what we say is important.

In short, the emphasis is less and less on manipulation and politicking. "How to win friends and influence people" is being reframed as "how to build teams" and "how to involve employees and value the diversity they bring." The shift moves from conventional office politics with its emphasis on "dressing for success" and "playing the game" toward "entrepreneurism," "flexibility," "creativity," and "courage."

Finally, we need to choose a pathway that emphasizes win-win agreements.

From Win-Lose to Win-Win

Leaders operate in a world riddled with conflict. In fact, leadership typically emerges in answer to a conflict—a situation where one party blocks the needs, goals, or actions of another. Skilled negotiation is an essential tool of leadership. This includes the ability to:

1. Reach satisfactory agreements for both parties.

2. Behave in a way that is principled, that does not seek personal gain at another's expense, but instead leaves the relationship intact or enhanced for future dealings.

3. Focus on common ground as a way of forming coalitions for mutual agreements.

4. Use fair, objective, mutually agreed-upon criteria to resolve differences.

5. Focus on satisfying important underlying needs on the part of both parties.

Approaching conflict management from this mindset truly requires releasing the more coercive "win-lose" stance typical of less powerful people.

In summary, the real test of leadership is the ability to change. The leader brings about new states or renews old conditions by enlisting or supporting others in the change process. To lead promotes renewal. When individuals and organizations fail to adopt this mindset, they can no longer respond to environmental threats and opportunities. They get stuck; they may even wither and die. Our life crises, then, are best understood as the proving ground for our ability to adapt. The critical lessons of leadership development are embedded in our lifelines. As we adapt to the challenges of our individual lives, we develop coping skills that allow us to avoid our own "extinction." When we change direction, try new approaches, or learn new coping skills, we engage in personal leadership. In the process, we may also lead others.

Leadership and Power

Janet Hagberg, in her book, *Real Power,* eloquently speaks of true leadership as "a willingness to be other than who the world wants you to be." Hagberg makes a distinction between leadership in general, and "true" leadership, which emerges at a critical developmental juncture for those who struggle with and resolve what she labels "a crisis of integrity." Janet's own crisis of integrity came when her husband suddenly left her while she was at (what seemed to be) the peak of her career as an international consultant. The trauma of this unexpected loss plunged her into the depths of despair, causing her to begin to question everything that had worked for her until that point in her life. As she pursued the long, torturous journey back from the depths of confusion and pain, she became aware of many important lessons—about herself, about life challenges, and about personal power. *Real Power,* a book that has positively affected many lives, including my own, stands as a testimony to Janet Hagberg's ability to exercise leadership through the sharing of ideas. In healing herself, she managed to help heal many "followers" in search of a path to personal power.

According to Hagberg's teaching, the evolution of leadership is tied to the individual's development of personal power as he or she resolves what Gail Sheehy refers to in her book *Passages* as "predictable adult crises." As a result, we lead differently at different stages of our development, based on our **internal** motivations at each stage. It is possible to live our lives fixed at any one stage, but to emerge as a true leader, or to achieve self-mastery, it is necessary to keep moving from one stage to the next.

The trick lies in leaving ourselves **open** to lessons our lives attempt to teach us. Only then will we clarify our values and determine what is important and what is insignificant at work, at home, in our communities. By paying attention to the choices we make at those critical times, we can note what worked well, what we would do differently next time, what innate strengths we have access to and what areas need to be strengthened. We will then be better positioned to seek out appropriate mentors, support networks, and other learning facilitators that are necessary for continued leadership development.

Some people are uncomfortable with the word "power." They attach negative connotations to the word because in their experience it has become synonymous with *coercion* or *manipulation.* They assume that when people use power someone always wins at the expense of another. This is not necessarily the case. Power can be positive or negative, depending on the source and on its application. When we act ethically and with integrity, when our actions are motivated by a concern for others, we position ourselves to use power in its most positive sense: **to achieve the goals of leadership, or to help people fulfill their needs.**

The willingness to engage in honest self-assessment, to examine our thoughts, feelings, and actions, holds the key to developing personal power and leadership effectiveness. Our thoughts, feelings and actions are the most important tools of leadership. This chapter will examine the relationships between power and leadership, and explore how our state of mind, as reflected in our thoughts and feelings, governs our power to act in ways that are consistent with good leadership.

Personal Power: The Fuel of Leadership

From my mid- to late-twenties, I spent many hours with college friends in truly inspiring brainstorming meetings (or "rap sessions" as we referred to them then). We were highly motivated and quite innovative in our thinking about ways to address the social and political issues of our time. We generated many ideas on ways to bring more social equity to our college campuses, ways to address pressing Third World issues, solutions for world peace, eradicating hunger and so forth.

I can still remember the frustration that followed when we would move from reasoning to the implementation phase. It always came back to money (which we didn't have), political clout (which we lacked), and credibility (which we hadn't yet earned).

At times, these frustrations would manifest themselves into campus demonstrations, as we banded together in support groups designed to relieve our feelings of anger and hopelessness. **The most important leadership lesson I learned from this experience in the sixties is that in the absence of real personal power, would-be leaders will resort to coercion. When people feel powerless, they eventually turn to force—the only form of power they perceive themselves as having.** In the short term this force or coercion may have the positive effect of drawing attention to the issues. Then, if the advocates of change are fortunate enough to attract into their ranks people who have "real power," their cause can be addressed effectively.

There can be no leadership without a power source. Power fuels leadership. The most well-conceived ideas or goals die if we do not have personal and/or organizational power to implement the concept.

Preparing ourselves for leadership means developing both sources of our power. Our personal power links our unique characteristics to the ways we have integrated our life experiences. This includes where we are in our spiritual development; the degree of self-esteem and confidence we embody; such personal character traits as honesty, consistency, discipline, and devotion to our life purpose and integrity; the ability to act in ways consistent with our stated values.

Organizational power is bestowed upon people by virtue of their level of expertise, titles, rank, connection with people of high status, membership in the "right" social groups, and so forth. Yet there are persons at high organizational levels who, because they **lack personal power or conviction, are unable to exercise leadership. They diminish themselves and their leadership capabilities by failing to develop themselves personally.**

As leaders, we promote change more effectively when we draw on both personal power (lessons learned from resolving life struggles) and organizational power (our position, expertise, and knowledge).

Most people I work with are fairly clear about ways to develop organizational power. They know the valued courses of study in their field, how to decipher what their companies reward and therefore how to climb the proverbial success ladder. They use this knowledge to set acceptable goals and engage in appropriate professional or managerial behaviors.

What is more elusive, I find, is how one develops personal power: how to make positive contributions based on individual conviction; how to be comfortable with being oneself in the workplace; how to exercise one's God-given talents for the enhancement of the larger community; how to feel comfortable about sharing one's thoughts and feelings, even in situations where these may be inconsistent with the "company line." **Yet, elusive or not, these abilities set the stage for the emergence of true leadership**. These qualities enable the leader to tell the truth as he or she sees it, to challenge the status quo, to achieve consistency between beliefs and actions, and to build and maintain **credibility** with followers.

The Power of Thought

In my consulting practice I meet many supervisors, managers, and professionals who lessen their leadership potential by "passing the buck upward." They claim: "The system won't let me," or "It's the folks at the top who are blocking our progress." These employees fail to realize that they too are "the system," that they too are part of "the leadership." Their chosen perspective erodes both their personal and organizational power.

When I counsel employees who release their power this way, I ask the question: "What do you have to offer that is valuable to your organization?" I get answers like "commitment," "expertise," "ideas," "feedback," "cooperation," and "compliance." **Unfortunately, people are not always aware of their power's worth.** It took blacks in Montgomery, and elsewhere, many years and a few courageous trailblazers to finally realize the one thing they had control over—that they could give or withhold—was compliance. When they ceased to comply by boycotting the buses, they empowered themselves to act. Anne Frank's detention by the Nazis is a most extreme example of an attempt at complete disempowerment. But even in her most dire circumstances, she never relinquished her power of thought. As a result, she continues to exercise leadership, inspiring us today.

Jean Fritz Chery, a Haitian artist born with no arms and hands, rose to his challenge of his physical disability, becoming an internationally known artist who won the 1981 United Nations' International Year of the Handicapped Artist Award. His success no doubt is tied to his thought patterns. According to Chery, "In a way, I see my handicap as affording me more possibilities. When I get tired of painting with my mouth, I shift to my left foot; when I'm tired of working with my left foot, I shift to my right foot. People with two arms and hands limit themselves. They only paint with one hand. And when that hand gets tired, they stop."

The Dynamics of Thoughts, Feelings, and Actions

To become our most powerful self requires honest self-examination. We must look at the ways we block ourselves from achieving our goals. One helpful exercise helps us pay attention to our **thoughts, feelings, and actions**. The table below gives examples of how powerless and powerful people think, feel and act.

Powerless Thoughts	Powerful Thoughts
"They won't let me."	"I choose not to."
"I am powerless."	"I can exert influence."
"They made me."	"I let them."
"I'm inferior."	"I'm pleased with myself."

Powerless Feelings	Powerful Feelings
Helpless	Confident
Hopeless	Hopeful
Dependent or co-dependent	Interdependent or independent
Undeserving	Deserving

Powerless Actions	Powerful Actions
Complaining	Stating expectations
Manipulating	Negotiating
Asking for permission	Giving self permission
Seeking validation from others	Being self-affirming
Blaming others	Accepting responsibility
Giving up	Exercising leadership

The journey inward begins with listening to the daily messages we send ourselves when faced with personal or professional challenges. Remember, our thought patterns shape our life choices. More important, they also help shape our subsequent experiences. Thus, the thoughts-feelings-actions dynamics outlined in the table above is a cyclical process. Thoughts evoke feelings which, in turn, activate behaviors. The way we process the impact of those behaviors creates new thoughts (or reinforces old ones).

Our external world (how we deal with challenges and people) reflects our inner world (what we think and feel). If we frequently think "That can't be done in this company," or "I'm too old to change directions in my life," we create a future shaped by those premises.

If we think people can't be trusted, then we operate from a position of fear and defensiveness. This usually evokes defensive responses from others, thereby confirming our negative thoughts. Similarly, if we think subordinates will lose respect for us if we reveal that we don't have all the answers, we set ourselves up to fail, because by indulging that thought, we are less likely to ask for their help or ideas. We might choose instead to work in the dark—making decisions without the necessary input from the work team.

Public speaking, the number one fear of Americans according to the *Book of Lists*, provides perhaps the best example of this point. A speaker whose thoughts turn to what could go wrong, instead of what would be most useful for his or her audience, is more likely to fail. Often public speakers approach the podium thinking, "I'm going to draw a blank," or "They'll probably ask me questions I can't answer." These **thoughts create feelings** of anxiety and self-doubt. These feelings trigger physical symptoms such as tense muscles, shaking hands, a tight throat, and "butterflies" in the stomach. The resulting **action** lacks focus on the audience's needs as the speaker muses on his or her own stress level. This naturally increases the possibility of drawing a blank, or fumbling through a difficult question to save face rather than admitting to a lack of information on a particular aspect of the topic (which, by the way, audiences can handle if it is done with integrity).

In leadership, as in all other aspects of life, our thoughts motivate our actions. If we concentrate on what could go wrong, we approach leadership from a position of powerlessness. This is a contradiction in terms, since power fuels leadership and leadership breeds power.

When social change advocates fail, it is often because they dwell more on what's lacking than on what's possible. By putting a disproportionate amount of energy into documenting bad things, they leave no energy for envisioning and attracting better conditions.

After a recent fund-raising dinner for a major civil rights organization, I left feeling depressed and hopeless, demotivated rather than "pumped up" for change. The reason? Both the keynote speaker and the executive director of the organization spent their entire speaking time revealing shocking statistics about the blight and hopelessness in our inner cities. While their content was accurate and the issues certainly worthy of attention, by focusing our thoughts on the negative side of the equation (what is lacking), and omitting the positive side of the equation (what is possible), they created feelings of despair, and were, therefore, unable to sign on new members for their change efforts.

This is often the impact some media elements have on young minds as reports highlight the negative for its sensational impact. Until the media learn to balance hopelessness with hope, they will never fully realize their potential to have a positive leadership impact on society.

I typically work with organizations that struggle with contemporary challenges like "downsizing" the workforce, or instituting new values such as "Total Quality" or "Customer First." In this work I notice that regardless of the nature of the business—government or industry, educational or non-profit agencies—**employees undergoing change experience a lot of pain**. Their thoughts and feelings run along the same patterns regardless of their job description or position in the organization. Typical thought patterns when faced with change include: "Things will never be the same again, how awful," or "I've seen new programs come and go; they never work," or "Do they (the top management) really know what they're doing?" Many also think: "The status quo (or the "good old days") was better; at least it was familiar and I knew what was expected of me." The feelings that accompany these thoughts include **disorientation, disempowerment, fear, and loss**.

Even in cases where the employees **agree** that the changes are necessary for survival, these thoughts and feelings create behaviors or actions
that may hamper the best leadership efforts.

What is most curious, though, is the fact that the very leaders themselves—the "champions" of the change effort, often allow the same
patterns of thoughts, feelings, and behaviors to dull their vision and
their enthusiasm. This creates a crisis within the crisis of change. Followers expect their leaders to act with courage, clarity, and conviction.
However, these are not qualities born of thoughts of powerlessness.

James Kouzes and Barry Posner in their excellent book, *The Leadership
Challenge*, make the point that the difference between managing
(maintaining a stable organization) and leading (creating a new state) is
that managing aims at "getting people to do," and leadership inspires
people "to want to do."

Unless the leader can eradicate negative thought patterns and visualize
the best possible future, it is unlikely that he or she can **get others
to *want* to go there!**

Modern medicine now acknowledges what we have known for centu-
ries: the mental attitude of patients is a critical factor in the healing
process. There is now scientific evidence that positive thoughts actually
release hormones that improve our immune system and our psycho-
logical outlook. The same healing process applies externally in our organizations when we interact powerfully with others through positive
purpose. Keeping fear, anger, and self-doubt within us is destructive.
When we learn how to release those thoughts and feelings, we tend to
create "healing" environments on our jobs, in our communities, and
in our personal relationships.

The leader's internal patterns of thoughts and feelings can be a major
force in inspiring positive thoughts, feelings, and followers. Then the art

of shared leadership activates, where all team members align behind a single vision and where all are then empowered through their actions to use their creativity to secure desired goals.

Thoughts are ideas or beliefs that we hold. Feelings are the "gut" reactions evoked by our thoughts. Here are some examples of contradictory thoughts held by different participants in my leadership training seminars:

"Work is natural."

"Most people want to avoid work."

"I can make a difference in this world."

"I can't make a difference in this world."

Imagine the feelings that accompany the thoughts listed above. The trainee who thinks "I can make a difference in this world" may feel powerful, challenged, proud, or useful, for example; while the trainee who thinks "I can't make a difference" may feel powerless, frustrated threatened, or angry.

If our thoughts center on what is possible, we create for ourselves and our followers, visions of a better future. This in turn engenders feelings of hope and commitment that will support the actions needed to create that future. **The ability to envision positive outcomes is the essence of leadership.** The challenge of **the journey inward** is to root out old thought patterns that inhibit our effectiveness and replace them with new ones.

The worksheets that follow will help you to identify your patterns of thoughts, feelings, and actions in different areas of your life. As you work through the exercises, pay attention to both the positive and negative aspects of your **inner world** of thoughts and feelings, and your **outer world** of behaviors or actions.

EXERCISE 1

Identify a recent success you had that involved activities with a family member or a friend, such as giving counsel or support of some kind. Answer the questions below as they relate to the event you identified.

1. **What thoughts motivated you as you acted in this situation?**

   _____

   _____

   _____

2. **What were your predominant feelings?**

   _____

   _____

   _____

3. **Describe your actions, what you accomplished and how.**

   _____

   _____

   _____

EXERCISE 2

Identify the most impressive success you have experienced at work. Pick something that you initiated or contributed to in a major way. Answer the questions below as they relate to the event you identified.

1. What thoughts motivated you as you worked on the project?

_____

_____

_____

2. What were your predominant feelings?

_____

_____

_____

3. Describe your actions, what you accomplished and how.

_____

_____

_____

EXERCISE 3

Reflect on your typical thought and feeling patterns when facing each of the situations described below.

Family Gatherings:

Thoughts   Feelings

_____

_____

_____

_____

Going to Work Each Day:

Thoughts   Feelings

_____

_____

_____

_____

Making a Major Purchase:

Thoughts   Feelings

_____

_____

_____

_____

Expressing Dissatisfaction to Your Boss:

Thoughts   Feelings

_____

_____

_____

_____

Expressing Dissatisfaction to Your Subordinate:

Thoughts   Feelings

_____

_____

_____

_____

Receiving Criticism from Another Person:

Thoughts   Feelings

_____

_____

_____

_____

Joining a New Group for the First Time:

Thoughts   Feelings

_____

_____

_____

_____

Asking for What You Want, or Wanting More:

Thoughts   Feelings

_____

_____

_____

_____

Now go back over your lists and look for themes in your thoughts and feelings. The following questions might help:

1. How have these thoughts and feelings shaped the *actions* you've taken in the past?

2. In what kinds of situations do you have positive attitudes? Negative attitudes?

3. What situations create the most stress for you? What kinds of behaviors are typical for you in those stressful situations. What role do your thoughts and feelings play?

4. How have your leadership behaviors been shaped positively and/or negatively by your own thoughts and feelings?

5. **What would you like to do differently as a result of these insights?**

6. **Now identify a negative thought you hold about yourself. List the THOUGHT, your FEELING in response to that thought and the BEHAVIORS or ACTIONS it evokes from you. Then rewrite the script by changing the negative thought into a positive affirmation. Rewrite the feelings and behaviors to flow from a positive affirmation. (Repeat this exercise any time you catch yourself engaging in negative or self-limiting thoughts.)**

PART III

THE
JOURNEY
OUTWARD

Dilemmas of Leadership

I work with leaders who consistently report that in today's climate, leadership has become a balancing act. The general consensus is that to be successful, a leader must be adept at making choices, often between two extremes on a continuum of possible behaviors. In this chapter I will outline a series of these dilemmas, and offer some suggestions on ways to achieve balance or maintain integrity in the face of each one.

DILEMMA 1: Balancing the need to act decisively with the need to empower team members. This dilemma is an important issue in the decision-making process. Basically, there are three approaches at a leader's disposal when making decisions.

The first approach is often labeled the **command** approach. Here the leader decides on a course of action and hands down that decision in "take it or leave it" fashion. The advantage of this efficient approach is that it works well when there is a crisis or when the situation dictates no room for negotiation. For example, in most organizations today, safety is never negotiable; the organization surveys its environment and develops a safety policy. Participants who adhere to the policy continue to be part of the organization, and those who don't face punitive actions or may no longer be part of the organization. The term "command decision" obviously comes from military jargon. In the heat of battle, a strong, decisive leader acts. Where there is much at stake, when people are in danger, followers expect the leader to act quickly in a forthright manner.

There are disadvantages to the command approach when applied inappropriately. It alienates people and does not allow for innovation. In situations calling for creativity, it would be an inappropriate option as it is limited by not incorporating the various views of people who may have expertise to lend to the decision-making process.

The second available option is called the **consultative** approach. This may be used in two ways. When the leader asks for input among followers but reserves the right to use or not to use that input, depending on the restraints that the leader may face, he or she uses the consultative approach. In using this approach, it is very important for the leader to make ground rules clear to the followers. Perhaps one of the most frequent mistakes in business meetings occurs when the leader gives the impression that he or she is gathering information in this consultative mode—that he or she wants the input and will use it—when, in fact, the leader has already made a tentative decision. The leader may then, upon receiving input, try to change the participants' view so that it fits the tentative decision already made. This of course alienates people, and poorly executes the consultative approach.

A second consultative approach engages participants in joint decision making. This means that the leader elicits input, while indicating a willingness to be flexible on his or her position, so the group can capitalize on its collective intelligence and experience. The advantages of using this consultative method? First, people feel included, and thus are more likely to commit to carry forth the decision. Second, the leader benefits from having the added input of those with direct line responsibility for areas within the leader's responsibility. The consultative method supports today's changing business climate because it also builds participatory involvement and team spirit.

The third approach to decision making is the **consensus** approach. This is where the leader says to the group, let's deliberate until we all reach agreement on the preferred course of action. While time consuming, and often difficult to achieve, this approach is useful where significant agreement or buy-in is required. Consensus decision-making goes beyond just collaboration to inspire workers to "own" the problem, "own" the solution, and therefore have a larger stake in the organization and its outcomes. There is rarely such a thing as 100 percent consensus. Leadership of consensus seeking may mean that everyone has had a chance to give their input, and those who don't fully agree are willing to go forward, having had their say. It is important to hold out for some form of consensus in situations where the stakes are high and risks could be costly.

All three approaches, command, consultative, and consensus, have their place in the leadership process. The dilemma for the leader is in deciding when to command and when to engage others. How does a leader to make this decision?

First of all, size up the situation and decide whether it represents a crisis. Ask for input from followers about what they perceive is needed in the situation. Often followers say to the leader, "We need you to make the decision. We need you to tell us what to do. We need you to be decisive and authoritative at this moment." At other times, followers say, "We need to express our feelings; we need to have input." So this decision making is an important step to take. Related to that step, leaders must ensure that once they decide which of the three decision-making approaches to use, they communicate that approach to the followers. Followers can handle it if, for example, they are told, "This is going to have to be a command decision; my hands are tied by the regulators," or "We're going to have to do this; it's the law." If, on the other hand, the leader says to the followers, "We're going to go the consultative route. I need your input and your ideas. I will work very hard to incorporate them," that too can be accepted if clearly expressed.

When delegating to followers, the leader must be sure to stipulate the delegated assignment and outline the degree to which it is delegated. In other words, does the leader want them to take the ball and run with it and not seek input at all unless there is a problem, or are they to periodically check with the leader to give progress reports, or are they fully responsible to the outcome? Again, if stated clearly, people can handle it. They know what is expected of them and will carry out the decision in a much more concrete way.

Finally, leaders must recognize that leadership doesn't work at one end or the other of a continuum, but moves freely up and down the continuum. The wise leader analyzes the risks involved, the skill level of the individuals, the situation itself, and then, based on that analysis, chooses the command, consultative, or consensus route for the situation. According to Dr. Mary Gail Biebel, a management consultant who specializes in leadership development for technical organizations, "The most important thing a leader must keep in mind during the decision-making process is the distinction between compliance and commitment. **The command approach gets people to act while the consultative or consensus approach can inspire them to want to act.**"

To make the appropriate decision-making choice with integrity means being clear about available choices, being clear about your intentions as the leader, and being honest and open to your followers about your actions. If you do this consistently, then, in most cases, you will get the support of co-workers whenever faced with this dilemma of choice.

EXERCISE 1

1. **Think of a decision you are likely to make in the near future. Pick one that is important. In the space below describe the nature of the decision.**

2. **Write down what you would decide to do if you had to make the decision on the spot, right now, with no time to think about it.**

3. **Decide whether the decision you just made instinctively would be enriched by input from others. If so, list the names of other people whose input would make the decision a better one.**

4. **Decide whether you should get this input consultatively, or by delegating it entirely to the other party or parties involved.**

5. **If you decided to go the consultative route, which of the two options would be most appropriate: getting others' input but reserving the right to make the final decision, or getting others' input and working with them to generate a joint decision?**

If you decided to go the delegative route, put a check mark next to the options offered below to indicate the level of your delegation.

_____ **Option 1:** Decide but check with me before you move forward on the decision.

_____ **Option 2:** Decide, implement the decision, but check with me at each stage of the way.

_____ **Option 3:** Decide, check in with me only if there are problems.

_____ **Option 4:** Make the decision and implement it. No further communication is necessary.

DILEMMA 2: Balancing personal vision with limited resources. It is safe to say that almost all of us work in a climate where, for various economic reasons, we are called upon to do more with less. As organizations become leaner, competition becomes fiercer and resources become more scarce; today's leader faces the challenge of balancing personal vision with limited resources. This dilemma calls forth a great deal of creativity and resourcefulness if the leader is to succeed in achieving goals. To attain his or her vision, the leader must encourage others to find new ways to reduce cost and to reach goals in the absence of sufficient financial and human resources.

Specifically, leaders must redefine how they view human resources. Training and joint decision making become key variables in creating a workforce adept and flexible in carrying out multiple functions where necessary. This may require a major shift in the leadership approach for leaders reluctant to develop the talents of workers.

Cultures that have successfully addressed issues of quality and competitiveness have learned this lesson. In Japan, for example, the average worker generates roughly thirty ideas per year that are listened to by management and taken into account where possible. In the United States, on the other hand, the average worker generates .07 suggestions per year. Americans tend to reward workers for grandiose suggestions or ground-breaking ideas, rather than daily rewarding minor suggestions for fine-tuning systems or improving the way we work. If the leader is to meet the challenge of balancing long-term vision with limited resources, he or she must begin to see the ideas of employees as a valued and currently under-used resource.

DILEMMA 3: Balancing the need to do things right with the need to do the right thing. Earlier in Chapter 4, I discussed the differences between managing and leading, citing the work of Warren Bennis and Burt Nanus and their often quoted, "Managers are people who do things right, and leaders are people who do the right thing." In pointing out this distinction, the authors also indicate one of the most trying leadership dilemmas: leaders struggle to understand how "doing the right things"—acting efficiently, rewarding behavior consistent with the company line, and discouraging or punishing behavior that is outside that line—combines with maintaining a well-run organization comfortable for all employees and customers.

On the other hand, the essence of **leadership is change**. Challenging the status quo can sometimes mean challenging the company line in order to foster innovation, find new ways to nurture breakthrough ideas, answer discontent among the workforce, or challenge the competition. Sometimes this means doing something right by the clients being served, though it may not be cost-effective or the most comfortable move for the organization to make. At those times the leader's dilemmas are whether to go out on a limb alone, how far out on the limb to go, or what to do if the risk causes failure.

Ralph Dickerson, president of the United Way of New York City, in talking about some of the more challenging leadership dilemmas of his career, sums up his understanding of how to resolve this "tug and pull" of managing versus leading, saying that when you take on a leadership role you must be "willing to be measured by the actions that you take." According to Dickerson, "You aren't leading if you aren't risking. When someone tells me I'm taking a risk by trying this path, I say, 'What else am I supposed to be doing?'" Dickerson goes on to explain that once he makes the decision to do what in his mind is the "right thing," he then relies on his staff, working in partnership with the community and the funding sources to manage the effort by doing things right.

DILEMMA 4: Balancing long-term goals with short-term progress. This is an important dilemma for leaders to think about because in leading a change effort, it is not unusual for those targeted by the change and for those involved in seeing the change through, to become disillusioned or frustrated if they are not able to see immediate results of their efforts. The wise leader understands this dilemma and plans "small wins," as they have been called in the literature on management and leadership training. That is, the leader sees to it that there are incremental steps taken toward the larger goal. The leader communicates that, "We're going to go from A to Z, but first let's concentrate on getting from A to B, from B to C, and so forth." At each step along the way, the leader remembers to celebrate those successes so that all persons involved in the change effort get a sense of progress and gain momentum with each success. Thus morale is less likely to be diminished, commitment is maintained, and the task does not seem so overwhelming that it saps the energy level and the spirit of the participants in change.

DILEMMA 5: Balancing the constraints of "traditional" organizational mindsets with the increasing need to value diversity. This is a relatively new dilemma of leadership, brought on by shifting workplace demographics and by the recognition that most organizations have not yet succeeded in creating a climate where all members are valued and empowered to perform to their best capacity. In fact, many in the field of leadership development would contend that our inability to exercise leadership in valuing diversity contributed to the steady decline of productivity we have experienced in the workplace over the past two or three decades. Many leaders who confront the dilemma of managing and valuing diversity find that their lack of experience and sophistication in dealing with the social distance between people who are different from each other impedes their ability to effectively motivate others and develop good interpersonal work relationships. One of the serious organizational consequences of this is that many minorities are not adequately included. As a result, they cannot develop and contribute all they are capable of bringing to the workplace. The resulting lack of trust and presence of awkwardness, presents problems of both productivity and creativity for minority and majority team members alike. To better manage this dilemma, today's leaders must develop skill in working effectively with people whose gender, culture, race, sexual orientation, socioeconomic background, or physical capabilities differ from their own. The challenge for the leader is to free himself or herself from operating out of a biased or stereotypical frame of reference. Because leaders are by definition "people in power," it is easy for them to slip into feeling comfortable with the status quo. Thus, they can easily avoid raising difficult issues related to differences or to the needs of people who are not empowered or not "in power." A leader's refusal to address these issues, prevents followers from fully participating in the leadership agenda.

In the words of R. Roosevelt Thomas, Jr., executive director for the Institute for Managing Diversity at Atlanta's Morehouse College, "In a country seeking economic advantage in a global economy, the goal of managing diversity is to develop our capacity to accept, incorporate, and empower the diverse human talent of the most diverse nation on earth. It's a reality. We need to make it our strength."

DILEMMA 6: Balancing the tension between ego and goals.

Because we're human we all live with the polarity of **ego** versus **goals: looking good versus doing good**. For example, if you were raised in an environment where you were constantly pressured by an overbearing or dominant parent, you may have developed an ego mechanism for coping with the anxiety that those behaviors triggered. For example, you may have learned to "tune out" the dominating parent. This behavior, as it gets transferred from situation to situation in order to protect your ego needs, would then be exhibited later in life to *anyone* who came on as strong, aggressive, or overbearing. So in the workplace or in a leadership context you might respond to a domineering colleague or subordinate using the same defense mechanism of tuning them out.

Psychotherapist Dr. Lois Dabney Smith, often asks her corporate clients who are wrestling with ego defensive problems to consider the following questions: "What are your goals in this situation? Is it more important that you get there or that you look good?" She offers the account of a senior manager in a Fortune 500 company who was a "real visionary."

Unfortunately, this man became increasingly angry and despondent and refused to produce in his new job because he felt he had a "window dressing" position. Yet, he admitted that it was possible to achieve his goals for the organization rather well from this vantage point. In fact, the position afforded him much flexibility in key areas. However, instead of pressing toward his leadership goals, he became obsessed with "looking good." Through a series of therapy sessions with Dr. Dabney Smith, he finally confronted his "ego versus goal" dilemma. He was then able to devise a systematic plan for deferring his immediate ego gratification and focusing on his long-term goals.

This implies then that **a major challenge of leadership is self-analysis, aimed at identifying the potential blind spots of our ego's needs that get in the way of our being most effective and responsive in the leadership role.**

DILEMMA 7: Balancing ethics with expediency. Leaders are routinely challenged by having to decide whether to honor ethics or act in the name of expediency. Often such a choice is tied to the cost considerations of a project, pressing time limits, or the pressure of producing quickly under dire circumstances. According to Dr. Peter Madsen, Director of the Center for Advancement of Applied Ethics at Carnegie Mellon University:

> The problem with the expedient decision is that it rests upon a "the end justifies the means" type of mentality. We know the ends do not

always justify the means and such thinking may in fact be unethical. The expedient decision always has hidden costs. Of course, there are many dramatic examples in our recent history of the devastating effects when the leadership chooses expediency over ethics. They range from the O-rings controversy at Morton Thiokol, leading to the space shuttle Challenger's disaster, to the unethical ways in which baby food manufacturers appeal to Third World consumers by dressing sales representatives in white, implying that they are health profession-als, while at the same time, failing to fully explain how to prepare and use the food in hygienic ways. Among the most dramatic of such examples is that of the "Pinto Case." The leadership of Ford Motor Company assigned a committee of engineers to review the engineering problem that led to the Pinto's gas tank explosions in rear-end colli-sions. The engineers commissioned the legal department to draw up a comparative analysis of what it might cost the company in lawsuits should they ignore the problem versus what it would cost to re-tool or re-design the car to eliminate the problem. Ford leadership, review-ing the results of the law department study, chose the most expedient or less expensive, less ethical route, deciding to leave the problem unattended. Of course, in the final outcome, when this case went to court, for the first time in history, a company was found guilty of "corporate murder."

In addressing the leadership dilemma of ethics versus expediency, Dr. Madsen offers six questions to be used as guidelines in determining whether your decision is an ethical one. These questions were adapted from the work of Laura L. Nash, as outlined in a 1981 *Harvard Busi-ness Review* article, entitled "Ethics without the Sermon."

1. Is my decision legal? Does it conform to policy and codes? Is it honest?

2. Can it pass a benefit harm test? Whom does it harm? Whom does it benefit? Can these be justified?

3. Does it treat everyone equally? If not, can the differences be justified?

4. Does it deny to anyone his or her rights?

5. Can I live with my decision? Does it rest comfortably on my conscience?

6. Can it pass the test of public scrutiny? Could I fully disclose it, without hesitation, to my supervisor or to a reporter from the *New York Times?*

Accepting the Leadership Challenge

Futurists and trend watchers like Alvin Toffler, John Naisbitt, and Marilyn Ferguson have convinced us that a new society, based on values and premises that suggest new paradigms for community building and leadership, is emerging. To paraphrase Toffler, the principles of standardization, synchronization and maximization that served us well during the Industrial Era are being replaced by new ones. In building our new communities we shift from **dependence and loyalty** in the workplace to **independence and employee satisfaction.** Our government is being transformed from **authoritarian** to a **semi-direct demography.** The focus of our economy has shifted from **land and capital** to **people and informa-tion,** and from **national** to **global** in scope. The **extended, rooted, or nuclear** family structure has evolved into highly **eclectic, flexible arrangements.** Health policy and health care organizations have **shifted from an institutionalized, symptom-driven, reactive stance to the proactive, preventative outlook,** typified by advocates of **wellness and self-care.**

These shifts in mindset are by no means panaceas for our social problems. They do, however, bring new leadership challenges and countless opportunities with them. In today's climate, **the journey inward** to leadership engages educators, business people, blue-collar workers, the clergy, politicians, professionals, students, and the growing number of unemployed in new ways that may be taxing or exhilarating, depending on the situation and the individual.

Creating a motivating environment in today's climate requires new levels of creativity and flexibility. Consider the following trends:

◆ **In some parts of the United States, prisons are being touted as the new growth industry.** One high-tech prison near Oregon, for example, holds 4,000 inmates, following a facility expansion. The community leaders were pleased that this change caused the community's population (which lay dormant for many years) to rise by more than 15 percent because the prison created 500 new jobs.

◆ **There is an ethics movement afoot in the United States.** This has been sparked by the disturbing news of insider trading, scandalous government contracting practices, questionable accounting practices and so forth. This movement, interestingly enough, brings together coalitions from different sectors of the community—schools, government, and corporate America— to promote ethics among the constituents they serve.

◆ **Many employees, especially women and minorities, formerly preoccupied with breaking through the "corporate glass ceiling" (barring their possible promotion to the top), now voluntarily leave to take on entrepreneurial ventures.** This reflects a new worker mindset that people are basically autonomous and do not have to have their needs met in the traditional workplace.

◆ **Each year six hundred thousand immigrants enter the United States legally, in addition to an estimated one million illegal immigrants.** The impact of immigration on our nation creates a series of domestic issues that affect education, business, and the overall community. How the leaders in various sectors choose to handle immigration policies will have a major impact on the size and make-up of the United States over the next decade.

◆ **Despite complaints that "the old work ethic is dying," Americans work longer hours today than they did twenty years ago.** The average American worker puts in forty nine hours per week, a 20 percent increase over 1970 figures. This may be partly due to the rise in small-business owners who tend to work longer hours. It is also somewhat attributable to what has been called the "baby-boomer work ethic," associated with the stereotypical driven, successful Wall Street yuppies of the '80s. Interestingly, while shrinking for the average American, leisure time in other parts of the world appears to be on the increase.

◆ **Product and service quality concerns have been shaping a new course for American industry, government and schools.** This recognizes the fact that we can no longer primarily rely on marketing and price differentiation to meet competition.

Add to the above sampling of trends changes in health care, increased environmental awareness and environmental spending (another new growth industry), the continued development and use of robotics, and the much quoted "Workforce 2000" demographics, and we get a rough picture of the incredible leadership challenges facing those who embark on the journey outward toward leadership.

Successful preparation for leadership in this arena, requires leaders understand and use premises such as the following to create the best motivating environment for themselves and others:

1. **Leadership is an act of service**. Rugged individualism, a cherished value in American society, can cloud our vision, causing us to forget that **leaders ultimately serve others**. The inner journey described in this book prepares the leader to build necessary coalitions or leadership teams to further that service. Private and public sector entities alike are beginning to realize what distinguishes successful organizations is their orientation to service. Success and competitiveness follow when the leadership vision takes into account the **needs** of the customer, constituents, employees, and other stakeholders. For example, People Express Airlines failed when it departed from this mindset, attempting to target the wrong customer base. Federal Express, in contrast, propelled itself into success by creating a culture driven by an almost obsessive focus on customer service. Leaders are people who chose to serve others.

2. **Leadership development is a lifelong process**. Our lives chronicle unfolding events, each with its special challenge, each with a special lesson—if we pay attention. This does not mean waiting passively for things to happen, however. In developing ourselves for leadership, we must actively seek out new experiences. Educators are becoming more aware of the need to begin leadership development in schools. In fact, leadership courses and hands-on leadership retreats are now part of the curriculum in more progressive schools. Corporations have long understood the importance of workplace learning in succession planning and human resource development. Currently, employee training and development in industry represents over two hundred billion

dollars per year. Each major initiative—such as Total Quality, Employee Involvement, or Customer Service Improvement—is bolstered by intensive training experiences designed to empower employees to take the lead in guaranteeing the anticipated outcomes. Likewise, performance management and career development strategies move employees into the right series of positions, giving exposure to personal and work-related experience that calls forth their best skills and leadership capabilities.

3. **Leadership development is both practical and spiritual in nature.** Because the study of leadership focuses on high ideals, creative pursuits and "visionary" thinking, it is easy to believe leadership is mysterious or mystical. It is neither. Leadership arises out of the practical need to address the everyday crises and challenges that accompany life. However, **true leadership does have a strong spiritual component. Our organizations are only as good as the people who run them. Preparation for effective leadership, then, involves preparing the soul of the leader.** We must continually examine our motives for leading. The responsibility of leadership shapes our own and others' lives—hopefully for the better. One of the most responsible tasks we face as leaders is that of promoting values. At the heart of most leadership initiatives is culture change. The human resource manager charged with changing the way employees greet and deal with customers affirms new values; the operations manager who decides to approach the bargaining unit with greater trust espouses new values; so is the community leader who decides to approach the school board with new ideas for school/community partnerships aimed at literacy.

In each of these cases, there is a good chance that there will be vigorous debates among different constituents on whether the right values are being promoted. Being spiritually attuned as a leader better equips us to "do the right thing" in each case. In one situation, the right thing may mean holding on to our conviction and forging ahead, prepared to pay the price for what we believe is right. In another situation, it may mean approaching a resolution that integrates important follower needs and values. In either case, our clarity of values and purpose, and the spiritual dimension of our personal and professional growth, make the difference.

4. **We are at our best as leaders when we are "balanced."**
   A favorite exercise in my leadership courses is one labeled "The Best Leader" exercise, adapted from the Kouzes and Posner book, *The Leadership Challenge.* The exercise simply requires trainees to think of the best leader they have ever personally known. They can pick a mentor, teacher, parent, boss, community leader, or friend—whomever they choose. Working first individually, then in groups of five, they are asked to list all the specific traits of their chosen "Best Leader." Invariably the trainees return with almost identical lists. Most interesting, however, is the content of the lists. In our culture, one would expect traits like "decisive," "aggressive," "a good planner," or "in control" to appear with regularity. Instead, the adjectives trainees list are decidedly in the arena of the "softer," more human traits: "caring," "supportive," "a good listener," "a good sense of humor," "honest," and "a good communicator" are among the most often recorded traits. In the discussion that ensues, trainees often point out that they expect leaders to demonstrate aggressiveness, decisiveness, good planning skills, and competence, but the "human" traits set the good leaders apart from the mediocre.

The most important lesson this exercise and my observations have taught me is that the best leaders are balanced. They are capable of being aggressive, yet fair; decisive, yet flexible (where appropriate); critical, yet caring; emphatic and persuasive in advocating their beliefs, yet able to listen and incorporate input from others. Ancient Taoism and Judaic and Christian religions, as well as great philosophers throughout history, have all taught the importance of balance. When Kenneth Blanchard and Spencer Johnson's *One Minute Manager* became perhaps the most widely read management guide, it was partly because it reaffirmed this universal truth so simply and convincingly. The promise? Tough, but nice; praise with reprimand; clear, firm goals and hard work with a sense of humor; and a belief that all people are potential winners. Perhaps American business is beginning to realize that it is off balance. We have focused excessively on the management side of leadership—driven by aggression, analysis, and control—for decades. We are beginning to shift our focus to the human side of leadership: service, employee involvement, team building, trust, and flexibility. This brings us to the next consideration.

5. **Men and women can make complementary contributions to leadership**. For decades management books taught us about very effective "masculine" models of management. This was appropriate since almost all major organizations were headed by men who bring to the workplace their set values and behaviors based on how they were socially acculturated. The masculine models, then, of management and leadership that appeared in our texts were based on the "warrior archetype," which rewarded such behaviors as decisiveness, aggressiveness, and "left-brain" logic. As Sally Helgesen points out in her book, *The Female Advantage,* traditionally feminine characteristics such as

"nurturing, mercy, participating in the growth of others, foster-
ing human connection . . . were all qualities that the warrior
could not afford to indulge or explore, lest they weaken his
resolve to compete. Thus the private domestic sphere over
which women reigned became the repository of humane and
caring value, while the world of work and politics flourished
by ruthless competition."

In more recent years, however, we have added to our understanding of leadership by including "feminine" models of leadership as well. The works of the late Alice Sargent, Carol Gilligan,
Judy Rosener, and Sally Helgesen, for example, document the
behaviors of women in the workplace who hold positions of
power and leadership. This is timely, given the influx of women
into the workplace over the past twenty years.

These studies provide compelling evidence that, like men,
women enter the workplace with their own set of values and
acculturation. For women this model of being nurturing, supportive, cooperative, and humane—**if allowed to surface**—
can be a powerful tool of leadership, especially given our growing orientation toward team building, employee involvement,
ownership, and customer service.

But, not all women feel confident enough to fully use themselves in this way. Also, not all women have been socialized in
traditional "feminine" values. Many are quite comfortable and
effective working with the "masculine" models of leadership. In
fact, during the '60s and '70s when women first began
to enter the workplace in large numbers, they more or less
emulated male models of leadership, regardless of their personal
orientation. Some went to great lengths to become clones of
men in their dress, demeanor, and approach to work. While this

may have been necessary as a transition phase for women, it is no longer the chosen mode. We see a reversal of this trend as women become more comfortable with personal power and leadership roles.

This gives us two viable models of leadership that together, form a more total picture and raise the possibility that **men and women can learn valuable lessons of leadership from each other in today's workplace. Together as men and women, we create meaningful synergy** at work if we value the specific orientations we bring. Most important, if, as individuals, whether male or female, we **allow ourselves to be who we are,** we incorporate those parts of ourselves that have been repressed by social conditioning. Thus, men can learn to value their intuitive, nurturing, humane side; while women can value the role of assertiveness, vision, and decisive strategy in the total structure of leadership. Through this balance we can all be heroic as we address life challenges at home, at work, and in our communities.

6. **Purpose and trust are the cornerstones of effective leadership.** This is true regardless of our gender, age, place of origin, race, or socioeconomic status. Purpose deals with conviction and the right goals. Trust is earned when we act in people's best interests, demonstrate consistency between what we say is important and what we do, and meet our goals competently. "Right" purpose and trust are also linked to honesty and a willingness to modify our position when proven wrong. Through introspection and assimilation of the lessons of our experiences, each of us discovers our **purpose.** As we learn what specifically we have to offer our communities where we live and work, **we must take steps to ensure that we carry forward our**

purpose with "trustworthiness" or integrity. This means
we must develop our self-esteem and self-worth, continually
clarifying our values so that our thoughts, feelings, and behaviors
are driven by positive motivations. This is how we move from
randomness to decisive action, creating synergy in our organizations and in our world.

Moving Inward . . .

◆ Take stock of where you've been and where you're
currently headed in your personal and work life.

◆ Identify critical roadblocks and pathways that have been
a part of your life's journey.

◆ Find the lessons and gifts behind the stories your life has
told you.

◆ Learn techniques for more fully tapping your leadership
potential.

◆ Develop action plans for your continual personal
empowerment.

Moving Outward . . .

◆ Develop the character of a wise leader: tell your truth, do what you say you believe in, be trustworthy, act with conviction and caring.

◆ Move from anger to forgiveness.

◆ Move from "nibbling" to empowerment.

◆ Move from rigidity to flexibility.

◆ Move from manipulation to authenticity.

◆ Move from win-lose to win-win.

◆ Move from powerless thoughts, to powerful actions.

ENJOY THE JOURNEY!

R E F E R E N C E S

Anderson, Nancy. *Work With Passion: How to Do What You Love for a Living.* New York, NY: Carroll and Graf Publishers, 1984.

Bennis, Warren and Burt Nanus. *Leaders.* New York, NY: Harper & Row, 1985.

Blanchard, Kenneth and Spencer Johnson. *The One Minute Manager.* New York, NY: William Morrow and Company, 1981.

Block, Peter. *The Empowered Manager.* San Francisco, CA: Jossey-Bass, Inc., Publishers, 1987.

Bridges, William. *Transitions: Making Sense of Life's Changes.* Reading, MA: Addison-Wesley, 1980.

Depree, Max. *Leadership is an Art.* New York, NY: Doubleday, 1989.

Ferguson, Marilyn. *The Aquarian Conspiracy.* Los Angeles, CA: Jeremy P. Tarcher, Inc., 1980.

Fritz, Robert. *The Path of Least Resistance: Principles for Creating What You to Create.* Salem, MA: Stillpoint Publishing, 1984.

Gardner, John W. *Leadership Papers, 1–12.* Washington, DC: Independent Sector, Leadership Studies Program, 1986–1988.

Harman, Willis, Ph.D. and Howard Rheingold. *Higher Creativity.* Los Angeles, CA: Jeremy P. Tarcher, Inc., 1984.

Hagberg, Janet O. *Real Power: Stages of Personal Power in Organizations.* Minneapolis, MN: Winston Press Inc., 1984.

Helgesen, Sally. *The Female Advantage.* New York, NY: Doubleday, 1990.

Jamison, Kaleel. *The Nibble Theory and the Kernel of Power.* New York, NY: Paulist Press, 1984.

Kanter, Rosabeth Moss. *The Change Masters.* New York, NY: Simon & Schuster, 1983.

Kelley, Robert E. *The Gold Collar Worker.* Reading, MA.: Addison-Wesley, 1985.

Kouzes, James M. and Barry Z. Posner. *The Leadership Challenge.* San Francisco, CA.: Jossey-Bass, Inc., Publishers, 1987.

Levinson, Daniel, et al. *Seasons of a Man's Life.* New York, NY: Ballantine, 1979.

Madsen, Peter, Ph.D. and Jay M. Shafritz, Ph.D. *Essentials of Business Ethics.* New York, NY: Meridian, 1990.

Naisbitt, John and Patricia Aburdene. *Reinventing the Corporation.* New York, NY: Warner Books, Inc.. 1985.

Sargent, Alice G. *The Androgynous Manager.* New York, NY: AMACOM, 1983.

Schein, Edgar H. *Organizational Culture and Leadership.* San Francisco, CA.: Jossey-Bass, Inc., Publishers, 1985.

Tichy, Noel M. and Mary Anne Devanna. *The Transformational Leader.* New York, NY: John Wiley & Sons, 1986.